Iowa
Assessments Success Strategies Level 14 Grade 8

DEAR FUTURE EXAM SUCCESS STORY

First of all, **THANK YOU** for purchasing Mometrix study materials!

Second, congratulations! You are one of the few determined test-takers who are committed to doing whatever it takes to excel on your exam. **You have come to the right place.** We developed these study materials with one goal in mind: to deliver you the information you need in a format that's concise and easy to use.

In addition to optimizing your guide for the content of the test, we've outlined our recommended steps for breaking down the preparation process into small, attainable goals so you can make sure you stay on track.

We've also analyzed the entire test-taking process, identifying the most common pitfalls and showing how you can overcome them and be ready for any curveball the test throws you.

Standardized testing is one of the biggest obstacles on your road to success, which only increases the importance of doing well in the high-pressure, high-stakes environment of test day. Your results on this test could have a significant impact on your future, and this guide provides the information and practical advice to help you achieve your full potential on test day.

Your success is our success

We would love to hear from you! If you would like to share the story of your exam success or if you have any questions or comments in regard to our products, please contact us at **800-673-8175** or **support@mometrix.com**.

Thanks again for your business and we wish you continued success!

Sincerely,
The Mometrix Test Preparation Team

Copyright © 2024 by Mometrix Media LLC. All rights reserved.
Written and edited by the Mometrix Test Preparation Team
Printed in the United States of America

ii

TABLE OF CONTENTS

INTRODUCTION _____ 1

STRATEGY #1 – PLAN BIG, STUDY SMALL _____ 2

STRATEGY #2 – MAKE YOUR STUDYING COUNT _____ 3

STRATEGY #3 – PRACTICE THE RIGHT WAY _____ 4

STRATEGY #4 – PACE YOURSELF _____ 6

TEST-TAKING STRATEGIES _____ 7

PRACTICE TEST _____ 11
    READING _____ 11
    WRITTEN EXPRESSION _____ 29
    MATHEMATICS _____ 45
    SCIENCE _____ 65
    SOCIAL STUDIES _____ 75
    VOCABULARY PRACTICE _____ 82
    SPELLING _____ 88
    CAPITALIZATION _____ 90
    PUNCTUATION _____ 95

PRACTICE TEST ANSWERS AND EXPLANATIONS _____ 99
    READING _____ 99
    WRITTEN EXPRESSION _____ 106
    MATHEMATICS _____ 109
    SCIENCE _____ 116
    SOCIAL STUDIES _____ 121
    VOCABULARY _____ 125
    SPELLING _____ 126
    CAPITALIZATION _____ 128
    PUNCTUATION _____ 130

HOW TO OVERCOME TEST ANXIETY _____ 133

ADDITIONAL BONUS MATERIAL _____ 139

iv

Introduction

Thank you for purchasing this resource! You have made the choice to prepare yourself for a test that could have a huge impact on your future, and this guide is designed to help you be fully ready for test day. Obviously, it's important to have a solid understanding of the test material, but you also need to be prepared for the unique environment and stressors of the test, so that you can perform to the best of your abilities.

For this purpose, the first section that appears in this guide is the **Success Strategies**. We've devoted countless hours to meticulously researching what works and what doesn't, and we've boiled down our findings to the five most impactful steps you can take to improve your performance on the test. We start at the beginning with study planning and move through the preparation process, all the way to the testing strategies that will help you get the most out of what you know when you're finally sitting in front of the test.

We recommend that you start preparing for your test as far in advance as possible. However, if you've bought this guide as a last-minute study resource and only have a few days before your test, we recommend that you skip over the first two Success Strategies since they address a long-term study plan.

If you struggle with **test anxiety**, we strongly encourage you to check out our recommendations for how you can overcome it. Test anxiety is a formidable foe, but it can be beaten, and we want to make sure you have the tools you need to defeat it.

Strategy #1 – Plan Big, Study Small

There's a lot riding on your performance. If you want to ace this test, you're going to need to keep your skills sharp and the material fresh in your mind. You need a plan that lets you review everything you need to know while still fitting in your schedule. We'll break this strategy down into three categories.

Information Organization

Start with the information you already have: the official test outline. From this, you can make a complete list of all the concepts you need to cover before the test. Organize these concepts into groups that can be studied together, and create a list of any related vocabulary you need to learn so you can brush up on any difficult terms. You'll want to keep this vocabulary list handy once you actually start studying since you may need to add to it along the way.

Time Management

Once you have your set of study concepts, decide how to spread them out over the time you have left before the test. Break your study plan into small, clear goals so you have a manageable task for each day and know exactly what you're doing. Then just focus on one small step at a time. When you manage your time this way, you don't need to spend hours at a time studying. Studying a small block of content for a short period each day helps you retain information better and avoid stressing over how much you have left to do. You can relax knowing that you have a plan to cover everything in time. In order for this strategy to be effective though, you have to start studying early and stick to your schedule. Avoid the exhaustion and futility that comes from last-minute cramming!

Study Environment

The environment you study in has a big impact on your learning. Studying in a coffee shop, while probably more enjoyable, is not likely to be as fruitful as studying in a quiet room. It's important to keep distractions to a minimum. You're only planning to study for a short block of time, so make the most of it. Don't pause to check your phone or get up to find a snack. It's also important to **avoid multitasking**. Research has consistently shown that multitasking will make your studying dramatically less effective. Your study area should also be comfortable and well-lit so you don't have the distraction of straining your eyes or sitting on an uncomfortable chair.

The time of day you study is also important. You want to be rested and alert. Don't wait until just before bedtime. Study when you'll be most likely to comprehend and remember. Even better, if you know what time of day your test will be, set that time aside for study. That way your brain will be used to working on that subject at that specific time and you'll have a better chance of recalling information.

Finally, it can be helpful to team up with others who are studying for the same test. Your actual studying should be done in as isolated an environment as possible, but the work of organizing the information and setting up the study plan can be divided up. In between study sessions, you can discuss with your teammates the concepts that you're all studying and quiz each other on the details. Just be sure that your teammates are as serious about the test as you are. If you find that your study time is being replaced with social time, you might need to find a new team.

Strategy #2 – Make Your Studying Count

You're devoting a lot of time and effort to preparing for this test, so you want to be absolutely certain it will pay off. This means doing more than just reading the content and hoping you can remember it on test day. It's important to make every minute of study count. There are two main areas you can focus on to make your studying count.

Retention

It doesn't matter how much time you study if you can't remember the material. You need to make sure you are retaining the concepts. To check your retention of the information you're learning, try recalling it at later times with minimal prompting. Try carrying around flashcards and glance at one or two from time to time or ask a friend who's also studying for the test to quiz you.

To enhance your retention, look for ways to put the information into practice so that you can apply it rather than simply recalling it. If you're using the information in practical ways, it will be much easier to remember. Similarly, it helps to solidify a concept in your mind if you're not only reading it to yourself but also explaining it to someone else. Ask a friend to let you teach them about a concept you're a little shaky on (or speak aloud to an imaginary audience if necessary). As you try to summarize, define, give examples, and answer your friend's questions, you'll understand the concepts better and they will stay with you longer. Finally, step back for a big picture view and ask yourself how each piece of information fits with the whole subject. When you link the different concepts together and see them working together as a whole, it's easier to remember the individual components.

Finally, practice showing your work on any multi-step problems, even if you're just studying. Writing out each step you take to solve a problem will help solidify the process in your mind, and you'll be more likely to remember it during the test.

Modality

Modality simply refers to the means or method by which you study. Choosing a study modality that fits your own individual learning style is crucial. No two people learn best in exactly the same way, so it's important to know your strengths and use them to your advantage.

For example, if you learn best by visualization, focus on visualizing a concept in your mind and draw an image or a diagram. Try color-coding your notes, illustrating them, or creating symbols that will trigger your mind to recall a learned concept. If you learn best by hearing or discussing information, find a study partner who learns the same way or read aloud to yourself. Think about how to put the information in your own words. Imagine that you are giving a lecture on the topic and record yourself so you can listen to it later.

For any learning style, flashcards can be helpful. Organize the information so you can take advantage of spare moments to review. Underline key words or phrases. Use different colors for different categories. Mnemonic devices (such as creating a short list in which every item starts with the same letter) can also help with retention. Find what works best for you and use it to store the information in your mind most effectively and easily.

Strategy #3 – Practice the Right Way

Your success on test day depends not only on how many hours you put into preparing, but also on whether you prepared the right way. It's good to check along the way to see if your studying is paying off. One of the most effective ways to do this is by taking practice tests to evaluate your progress. Practice tests are useful because they show exactly where you need to improve. Every time you take a practice test, pay special attention to these three groups of questions:

- The questions you got wrong
- The questions you had to guess on, even if you guessed right
- The questions you found difficult or slow to work through

This will show you exactly what your weak areas are, and where you need to devote more study time. Ask yourself why each of these questions gave you trouble. Was it because you didn't understand the material? Was it because you didn't remember the vocabulary? Do you need more repetitions on this type of question to build speed and confidence? Dig into those questions and figure out how you can strengthen your weak areas as you go back to review the material.

Additionally, many practice tests have a section explaining the answer choices. It can be tempting to read the explanation and think that you now have a good understanding of the concept. However, an explanation likely only covers part of the question's broader context. Even if the explanation makes perfect sense, **go back and investigate** every concept related to the question until you're positive you have a thorough understanding.

As you go along, keep in mind that the practice test is just that: practice. Memorizing these questions and answers will not be very helpful on the actual test because it is unlikely to have any of the same exact questions. If you only know the right answers to the sample questions, you won't be prepared for the real thing. **Study the concepts** until you understand them fully, and then you'll be able to answer any question that shows up on the test.

It's important to wait on the practice tests until you're ready. If you take a test on your first day of study, you may be overwhelmed by the amount of material covered and how much you need to learn. Work up to it gradually.

On test day, you'll need to be prepared for answering questions, managing your time, and using the test-taking strategies you've learned. It's a lot to balance, like a mental marathon that will have a big impact on your future. Like training for a marathon, you'll need to start slowly and work your way up. When test day arrives, you'll be ready.

Start with the strategies you've read in the first two Success Strategies—plan your course and study in the way that works best for you. If you have time, consider using multiple study resources to get different approaches to the same concepts. It can be helpful to see difficult concepts from more than one angle. Then find a good source for practice tests. Many times, the test website will suggest potential study resources or provide sample tests.

Practice Test Strategy

If you're able to find at least three practice tests, we recommend this strategy:

UNTIMED AND OPEN-BOOK PRACTICE

Take the first test with no time constraints and with your notes and study guide handy. Take your time and focus on applying the strategies you've learned.

TIMED AND OPEN-BOOK PRACTICE

Take the second practice test open-book as well, but set a timer and practice pacing yourself to finish in time.

TIMED AND CLOSED-BOOK PRACTICE

Take any other practice tests as if it were test day. Set a timer and put away your study materials. Sit at a table or desk in a quiet room, imagine yourself at the testing center, and answer questions as quickly and accurately as possible.

Keep repeating timed and closed-book tests on a regular basis until you run out of practice tests or it's time for the actual test. Your mind will be ready for the schedule and stress of test day, and you'll be able to focus on recalling the material you've learned.

Strategy #4 – Pace Yourself

Once you're fully prepared for the material on the test, your biggest challenge on test day will be managing your time. Just knowing that the clock is ticking can make you panic even if you have plenty of time left. Work on pacing yourself so you can build confidence against the time constraints of the exam. Pacing is a difficult skill to master, especially in a high-pressure environment, so **practice is vital**.

Set time expectations for your pace based on how much time is available. For example, if a section has 60 questions and the time limit is 30 minutes, you know you have to average 30 seconds or less per question in order to answer them all. Although 30 seconds is the hard limit, set 25 seconds per question as your goal, so you reserve extra time to spend on harder questions. When you budget extra time for the harder questions, you no longer have any reason to stress when those questions take longer to answer.

Don't let this time expectation distract you from working through the test at a calm, steady pace, but keep it in mind so you don't spend too much time on any one question. Recognize that taking extra time on one question you don't understand may keep you from answering two that you do understand later in the test. If your time limit for a question is up and you're still not sure of the answer, mark it and move on, and come back to it later if the time and the test format allow. If the testing format doesn't allow you to return to earlier questions, just make an educated guess; then put it out of your mind and move on.

On the easier questions, be careful not to rush. It may seem wise to hurry through them so you have more time for the challenging ones, but it's not worth missing one if you know the concept and just didn't take the time to read the question fully. Work efficiently but make sure you understand the question and have looked at all of the answer choices, since more than one may seem right at first.

Even if you're paying attention to the time, you may find yourself a little behind at some point. You should speed up to get back on track, but do so wisely. Don't panic; just take a few seconds less on each question until you're caught up. Don't guess without thinking, but do look through the answer choices and eliminate any you know are wrong. If you can get down to two choices, it is often worthwhile to guess from those. Once you've chosen an answer, move on and don't dwell on any that you skipped or had to hurry through. If a question was taking too long, chances are it was one of the harder ones, so you weren't as likely to get it right anyway.

On the other hand, if you find yourself getting ahead of schedule, it may be beneficial to slow down a little. The more quickly you work, the more likely you are to make a careless mistake that will affect your score. You've budgeted time for each question, so don't be afraid to spend that time. Practice an efficient but careful pace to get the most out of the time you have.

Test-Taking Strategies

This section contains a list of test-taking strategies that you may find helpful as you work through the test. By taking what you know and applying logical thought, you can maximize your chances of answering any question correctly!

It is very important to realize that every question is different and every person is different: no single strategy will work on every question, and no single strategy will work for every person. That's why we've included all of them here, so you can try them out and determine which ones work best for different types of questions and which ones work best for you.

Question Strategies

⊘ READ CAREFULLY

Read the question and the answer choices carefully. Don't miss the question because you misread the terms. You have plenty of time to read each question thoroughly and make sure you understand what is being asked. Yet a happy medium must be attained, so don't waste too much time. You must read carefully and efficiently.

⊘ CONTEXTUAL CLUES

Look for contextual clues. If the question includes a word you are not familiar with, look at the immediate context for some indication of what the word might mean. Contextual clues can often give you all the information you need to decipher the meaning of an unfamiliar word. Even if you can't determine the meaning, you may be able to narrow down the possibilities enough to make a solid guess at the answer to the question.

⊘ PREFIXES

If you're having trouble with a word in the question or answer choices, try dissecting it. Take advantage of every clue that the word might include. Prefixes can be a huge help. Usually, they allow you to determine a basic meaning. *Pre-* means before, *post-* means after, *pro-* is positive, *de-* is negative. From prefixes, you can get an idea of the general meaning of the word and try to put it into context.

⊘ HEDGE WORDS

Watch out for critical hedge words, such as *likely, may, can, sometimes, often, almost, mostly, usually, generally, rarely,* and *sometimes.* Question writers insert these hedge phrases to cover every possibility. Often an answer choice will be wrong simply because it leaves no room for exception. Be on guard for answer choices that have definitive words such as *exactly* and *always.*

⊘ SWITCHBACK WORDS

Stay alert for *switchbacks.* These are the words and phrases frequently used to alert you to shifts in thought. The most common switchback words are *but, although,* and *however.* Others include *nevertheless, on the other hand, even though, while, in spite of, despite,* and *regardless of.* Switchback words are important to catch because they can change the direction of the question or an answer choice.

7

Copyright © Mometrix Media. You have been licensed one copy of this document for personal use only. Any other reproduction or redistribution is strictly prohibited. All rights reserved.
This content is provided for test preparation purposes only and does not imply an endorsement by Mometrix of any particular political, scientific, or religious point of view.

⊘ FACE VALUE

When in doubt, use common sense. Accept the situation in the problem at face value. Don't read too much into it. These problems will not require you to make wild assumptions. If you have to go beyond creativity and warp time or space in order to have an answer choice fit the question, then you should move on and consider the other answer choices. These are normal problems rooted in reality. The applicable relationship or explanation may not be readily apparent, but it is there for you to figure out. Use your common sense to interpret anything that isn't clear.

Answer Choice Strategies

⊘ ANSWER SELECTION

The most thorough way to pick an answer choice is to identify and eliminate wrong answers until only one is left, then confirm it is the correct answer. Sometimes an answer choice may immediately seem right, but be careful. The test writers will usually put more than one reasonable answer choice on each question, so take a second to read all of them and make sure that the other choices are not equally obvious. As long as you have time left, it is better to read every answer choice than to pick the first one that looks right without checking the others.

⊘ ANSWER CHOICE FAMILIES

An answer choice family consists of two (in rare cases, three) answer choices that are very similar in construction and cannot all be true at the same time. If you see two answer choices that are direct opposites or parallels, one of them is usually the correct answer. For instance, if one answer choice says that quantity x increases and another either says that quantity x decreases (opposite) or says that quantity y increases (parallel), then those answer choices would fall into the same family. An answer choice that doesn't match the construction of the answer choice family is more likely to be incorrect. Most questions will not have answer choice families, but when they do appear, you should be prepared to recognize them.

⊘ ELIMINATE ANSWERS

Eliminate answer choices as soon as you realize they are wrong, but make sure you consider all possibilities. If you are eliminating answer choices and realize that the last one you are left with is also wrong, don't panic. Start over and consider each choice again. There may be something you missed the first time that you will realize on the second pass.

⊘ AVOID FACT TRAPS

Don't be distracted by an answer choice that is factually true but doesn't answer the question. You are looking for the choice that answers the question. Stay focused on what the question is asking for so you don't accidentally pick an answer that is true but incorrect. Always go back to the question and make sure the answer choice you've selected actually answers the question and is not merely a true statement.

⊘ EXTREME STATEMENTS

In general, you should avoid answers that put forth extreme actions as standard practice or proclaim controversial ideas as established fact. An answer choice that states the "process should be used in certain situations, if..." is much more likely to be correct than one that states the "process should be discontinued completely." The first is a calm rational statement and doesn't even make a definitive, uncompromising stance, using a hedge word *if* to provide wiggle room, whereas the second choice is far more extreme.

⊘ BENCHMARK

As you read through the answer choices and you come across one that seems to answer the question well, mentally select that answer choice. This is not your final answer, but it's the one that will help you evaluate the other answer choices. The one that you selected is your benchmark or standard for judging each of the other answer choices. Every other answer choice must be compared to your benchmark. That choice is correct until proven otherwise by another answer choice beating it. If you find a better answer, then that one becomes your new benchmark. Once you've decided that no other choice answers the question as well as your benchmark, you have your final answer.

⊘ PREDICT THE ANSWER

Before you even start looking at the answer choices, it is often best to try to predict the answer. When you come up with the answer on your own, it is easier to avoid distractions and traps because you will know exactly what to look for. The right answer choice is unlikely to be word-for-word what you came up with, but it should be a close match. Even if you are confident that you have the right answer, you should still take the time to read each option before moving on.

General Strategies

⊘ TOUGH QUESTIONS

If you are stumped on a problem or it appears too hard or too difficult, don't waste time. Move on! Remember though, if you can quickly check for obviously incorrect answer choices, your chances of guessing correctly are greatly improved. Before you completely give up, at least try to knock out a couple of possible answers. Eliminate what you can and then guess at the remaining answer choices before moving on.

⊘ CHECK YOUR WORK

Since you will probably not know every term listed and the answer to every question, it is important that you get credit for the ones that you do know. Don't miss any questions through careless mistakes. If at all possible, try to take a second to look back over your answer selection and make sure you've selected the correct answer choice and haven't made a costly careless mistake (such as marking an answer choice that you didn't mean to mark). This quick double check should more than pay for itself in caught mistakes for the time it costs.

⊘ PACE YOURSELF

It's easy to be overwhelmed when you're looking at a page full of questions; your mind is confused and full of random thoughts, and the clock is ticking down faster than you would like. Calm down and maintain the pace that you have set for yourself. Especially as you get down to the last few minutes of the test, don't let the small numbers on the clock make you panic. As long as you are on track by monitoring your pace, you are guaranteed to have time for each question.

⊘ DON'T RUSH

It is very easy to make errors when you are in a hurry. Maintaining a fast pace in answering questions is pointless if it makes you miss questions that you would have gotten right otherwise. Test writers like to include distracting information and wrong answers that seem right. Taking a little extra time to avoid careless mistakes can make all the difference in your test score. Find a pace that allows you to be confident in the answers that you select.

⏱ Keep Moving

Panicking will not help you pass the test, so do your best to stay calm and keep moving. Taking deep breaths and going through the answer elimination steps you practiced can help to break through a stress barrier and keep your pace.

Final Notes

The combination of a solid foundation of content knowledge and the confidence that comes from practicing your plan for applying that knowledge is the key to maximizing your performance on test day. As your foundation of content knowledge is built up and strengthened, you'll find that the strategies included in this chapter become more and more effective in helping you quickly sift through the distractions and traps of the test to isolate the correct answer.

Now that you're preparing to move forward into the test content chapters of this book, be sure to keep your goal in mind. As you read, think about how you will be able to apply this information on the test. If you've already seen sample questions for the test and you have an idea of the question format and style, try to come up with questions of your own that you can answer based on what you're reading. This will give you valuable practice applying your knowledge in the same ways you can expect to on test day.

Good luck and good studying!

Practice Test

Reading

Reading well is one of the most important skills you can cultivate. No matter what you hope to do with your life when you're an adult, being a good reader will make it easier for you to accomplish, and will help you be better at it. Of course, you'll also do much better in school if you have excellent reading skills, because digesting and retaining written information are two of the main components of learning practically any subject. Of course, reading for pleasure is its own reward, and can enrich your life in many different ways. This exercise will help you improve your reading skills. You'll be given a passage to read, and then you'll be asked several questions about it. Take your time and do your best, in order for you to get the most out of this review.

Questions 1 -12 pertain to the following passages:

Call of the Wild by Jack London

Buck did not read the newspapers, or he would have known that trouble was brewing, not alone for himself, but for every tide-water dog, strong of muscle and with warm, long
5 hair, from Puget Sound to San Diego. Because men, groping in the Arctic darkness, had found a yellow metal, and because steamship and transportation companies were booming the find, thousands of men were rushing into
10 the Northland. These men wanted dogs, and the dogs they wanted were heavy dogs, with strong muscles by which to toil, and furry coats to protect them from the frost.

Buck lived at a big house in the sun-kissed
15 Santa Clara Valley. Judge Miller's place, it was called. It stood back from the road, half hidden among the trees, through which glimpses could be caught of the wide cool veranda that ran around its four sides. The
20 house was approached by gravelled driveways which wound about through wide-spreading lawns and under the interlacing boughs of tall poplars. At the rear things were on even a more spacious scale than at the
25 front. There were great stables, where a dozen grooms and boys held forth, rows of vine-clad servants' cottages, an endless and orderly array of outhouses, long grape arbors, green pastures, orchards, and berry patches.
30 Then there was the pumping plant for the artesian well, and the big cement tank where Judge Miller's boys took their morning plunge and kept cool in the hot afternoon.

And over this great demesne Buck ruled.
35 Here he was born, and here he had lived the four years of his life. It was true, there were other dogs, there could not but be other dogs on so vast a place, but they did not count. They came and went, resided in the populous
40 kennels, or lived obscurely in the recesses of the house after the fashion of Toots, the Japanese pug, or Ysabel, the Mexican hairless,—strange creatures that rarely put nose out of doors or set foot to ground. On the
45 other hand, there were the fox terriers, a score of them at least, who yelped fearful promises at Toots and Ysabel looking out of the windows at them and protected by a legion of housemaids armed with brooms and
50 mops.

But Buck was neither house-dog nor kennel-dog. The whole realm was his. He plunged into the swimming tank or went hunting with the Judge's sons; he escorted
55 Mollie and Alice, the Judge's daughters, on long twilight or early morning rambles; on wintry nights he lay at the Judge's feet before the roaring library fire; he carried the Judge's grandsons on his back, or rolled them in the

11

Copyright © Mometrix Media. You have been licensed one copy of this document for personal use only. Any other reproduction or redistribution is strictly prohibited. All rights reserved.
This content is provided for test preparation purposes only and does not imply an endorsement by Mometrix of any particular political, scientific, or religious point of view.

60 grass, and guarded their footsteps through wild adventures down to the fountain in the stable yard, and even beyond, where the paddocks were, and the berry patches. Among the terriers he stalked imperiously,
65 and Toots and Ysabel he utterly ignored, for he was king,—king over all creeping, crawling, flying things of Judge Miller's place, humans included.

His father, Elmo, a huge St. Bernard, had
70 been the Judge's inseparable companion, and Buck bid fair to follow in the way of his father. He was not so large,—he weighed only one hundred and forty pounds,—for his mother, Shep, had been a Scotch shepherd dog.
75 Nevertheless, one hundred and forty pounds, to which was added the dignity that comes of good living and universal respect, enabled him to carry himself in right royal fashion. During the four years since his puppyhood he
80 had lived the life of a sated aristocrat; he had a fine pride in himself, was even a trifle egotistical, as country gentlemen sometimes become because of their insular situation. But he had saved himself by not becoming a mere
85 pampered house-dog. Hunting and kindred outdoor delights had kept down the fat and hardened his muscles; and to him, as to the cold-tubbing races, the love of water had been a tonic and a health preserver.

90 And this was the manner of dog Buck was in the fall of 1897, when the Klondike strike dragged men from all the world into the frozen North. But Buck did not read the newspapers, and he did not know that
95 Manuel, one of the gardener's helpers, was an undesirable acquaintance. Manuel had one besetting sin. He loved to play Chinese lottery. Also, in his gambling, he had one besetting weakness—faith in a system; and this made
100 his damnation certain. For to play a system requires money, while the wages of a gardener's helper do not lap over the needs of a wife and numerous progenies.

The Judge was at a meeting of the Raisin
105 Growers' Association, and the boys were busy organizing an athletic club, on the memorable night of Manuel's treachery. No one saw him and Buck go off through the orchard on what Buck imagined was merely a stroll. And with
110 the exception of a solitary man, no one saw them arrive at the little flag station known as College Park. This man talked with Manuel, and money chinked between them.

1. What is the purpose of paragraphs 2-5?

a. To introduce all of the story's characters
b. To show Buck's personality
c. To introduce Buck
d. To show Buck's affection for Toots and Ysabel

2. Which sentence or phrase shows Buck's attitude about Judge Miller's place?

a. They came and went, resided in the populous kennels, or lived obscurely in the recesses of the house
b. The whole realm was his
c. He had a fine pride in himself
d. And to him, as to the cold-tubbing races, the love of water had been a tonic and a health preserver

3. The author uses the detail in paragraph 1 to

a. Describe Buck's life
b. Foreshadow Buck's story
c. Describe the story's setting
d. Introduce the story's villain

4. What is the significance of the Klondike strike in 1897?

a. It will lead to changes in Buck's life
b. It will cause more dogs to move to Judge Miller's place
c. It changed Elmo's life
d. It caused the Raisin Growers' Association to meet more frequently

5. The use of the word *imperiously* in paragraph four helps the reader know that Buck feels

a. Scared
b. Angry
c. Happy
d. Regal

6. The author organizes this selection mainly by

a. Describing Buck's life in the order in which it happened
b. Outlining Buck's history
c. Showing Buck's life and then showing a moment of change
d. Comparing Buck's life at Judge Miller's place to what came afterwards

7. Which answer choice best describes the purpose of the selection?

a. To set up a story by providing background information
b. To show Buck in a moment of heroism
c. To give details about the Klondike strike
d. To introduce all the dogs that live at Judge Miller's

8. In the future, Buck will probably
   a. Continue to act like the king of Judge Miller's place
   b. Reunite with his father, Elmo, and his mother, Shep
   c. Leave Judge Miller's place against his will
   d. Spend more time in the garden

9. This selection is part of a longer work. Based on the selection, what might be a theme of the larger work?
   a. Change
   b. Family
   c. Hard work
   d. Relationships

10. Paragraph 2 is mostly about:
    a. The Santa Clara Valley
    b. Judge Miller's place
    c. Buck's lifestyle
    d. The Klondike strike

11. Which sentence from the passage foreshadows the rest of the story?
    a. And over this great demesne Buck ruled
    b. These men wanted dogs, and the dogs they wanted were heavy dogs, with strong muscles by which to toil, and furry coats to protect them from the frost
    c. His father, Elmo, a huge St. Bernard, had been the Judge's inseparable companion and Buck bid fair to follow in the way of his father
    d. But he had saved himself by not becoming a mere pampered house-dog

12. What's the most logical explanation why Buck doesn't read the newspapers?
    a. He's not interested in current events
    b. He's busy exploring Judge Miller's place
    c. The Raisin Growers' Association takes all his time
    d. He's a dog

Questions 13 – 16 pertain to the following passage:

Andy Grant's Pluck by Horatio Alger

(1) The house and everything about it seemed just as it did when he left at the beginning of the school term. But Andy looked at them with different eyes.

(2) Then he had been in good spirits, eager to return to his school work.

Now something had happened, he did not yet know what.

(3) Mrs. Grant was in the back part of the house, and Andy was in the sitting room before she was fully aware of his presence. Then she came in from the kitchen, where she was preparing supper.

(4) Her face seemed careworn, but there was a smile upon it as she greeted her son.

(5) "Then you got my telegram?" she said. "I didn't think you would be here so soon."

(6) "I started at once, mother, for I felt anxious. What has happened? Are you all well?"

(7) "Yes, thank God, we are in fair health, but we have met with misfortune."

(8) "What is it?"

(9) "Nathan Lawrence, cashier of the bank in Benton, has disappeared with twenty thousand dollars of the bank's money."

(10) "What has that to do with father? He hasn't much money in that bank."

(11) "Your father is on Mr. Lawrence's bond to the amount of six thousand dollars."

(12) "I see," answered Andy, gravely, "How much will he lose?"

(13) "The whole of it."

(14) This, then, was what had happened. To a man in moderate circumstances, it must needs be a heavy blow.

(15) "I suppose it will make a great difference?" said Andy, inquiringly.

(16) "You can judge. Your father's property consists of this farm and three thousand dollars in government bonds. It will be necessary to sacrifice the bonds and place a mortgage of three thousand dollars on the farm."

(17) "How much is the farm worth?"

(18) "Not over six thousand dollars."

(19) "Then father's property is nearly all swept away."

(20) "Yes," said his mother, sadly. "Hereafter he will receive no help from outside interest, and will, besides, have to pay interest on a mortgage of three thousand dollars, at six per cent."

(21) "One hundred and eighty dollars."

(22) "Yes."

(23) "Altogether, then, it will diminish our income by rather more than three hundred dollars."

(24) "Yes, Andy."

(25) "That is about what my education has been costing father," said Andy, in a low voice.

(26) He began to see how this misfortune was going to affect him.

(27) "I am afraid," faltered Mrs. Grant, "that you will have to leave school."

(28) "Of course I must," said Andy, speaking with a cheerfulness which he did not feel. "And in place of going to college I must see how I can help father bear this burden."

(29) "It will be very hard upon you, Andy," said his mother, in a tone of sympathy.

(30) "I shall be sorry, of course, mother; but there are plenty of boys who don't go to college. I shall be no worse off than they."

(31) "I am glad you bear the disappointment so well, Andy. It is of you your father and I have thought chiefly since the blow fell upon us."

(32) "Who will advance father the money on mortgage, mother?"

(33) "Squire Carter has expressed a willingness to do so. He will be here this evening to talk it over."

(34) "I am sorry for that, mother. He is a hard man. If there is a chance to take advantage of father, he won't hesitate to do it."

13. As it used in paragraph 1, the phrase *different eyes* means which of the following?
   a. Andy's eyes have changed color
   b. Andy now wears glasses
   c. Andy sees that the mood in the house has changed
   d. Andy is happy to be home

14. Read this sentence from paragraph 14:

   To a man in moderate circumstances, it must needs be a heavy blow.

The author uses the metaphor *a heavy blow* to indicate which of the following?
   a. Andy's father is in a difficult situation
   b. Andy won't be able to go back to school
   c. Andy's father has lost over six thousand dollars
   d. Andy is disappointed about his family's problems

15. Which of these is the best summary of the selection?
   a. Andy Grant comes home from school and discovers that his father has won six thousand dollars. He will use the money to buy equipment for the farm. Andy finds out that he will need to leave school in order to help his father on the farm and work for Squire Carter
   b. Andy Grant goes home and discovers that his family has fallen upon misfortune. Nathan Lawrence, the bank's cashier, has stolen twenty thousand dollars of Andy's father's money. Now that Andy's family has lost so much money, they won't be able to pay for his education and he'll have to leave school
   c. Andy Grant's father has lost six thousand dollars because Nathan Lawrence stole it. This loss will cost Andy's family a lot of money. Since Andy's family pays $300 a month for his school, he will have to stop going to school. Andy is very cheerful that he doesn't have to go to school. He decides to work for Squire Carter in order to help his family
   d. Andy Grant's family has suffered a misfortune because the bank's cashier stole money, some of which belonged to Andy's father. Without the money, Andy's family will have trouble paying its bills, including Andy's school bills. Andy will have to stop going to school. Furthermore, his father will have to borrow money

16. What phrase or sentence from the selection best shows Andy's feelings about having to leave school?
   a. He began to see how this misfortune was going to affect him
   b. Speaking with a cheerfulness which he did not feel
   c. And in place of going to college I must see how I can help father bear this burden
   d. I am sorry for that, mother

Questions 17 – 21 pertain to the following passage:

The Telegraph Boy by Horatio Alger

(1) Our hero found himself in a dirty apartment, provided with a bar, over which was a placard, inscribed:—

(2) "FREE LUNCH."

(3) "How much money have you got, Frank?" inquired Montagu Percy.

(4) "Twenty-five cents."

(5) "Lunch at this establishment is free," said Montagu; "but you are expected to order some drink. What will you have?"

(6) "I don't care for any drink except a glass of water."

(7) "All right; I will order for you, as the rules of the establishment require it; but I will drink your glass myself. Eat whatever you like."

(8) Frank took a sandwich from a plate on the counter and ate it with relish, for he was hungry. Meanwhile his companion emptied the two glasses, and ordered another.

(9) "Can you pay for these drinks?" asked the bar-tender, suspiciously.

(10) "Sir, I never order what I cannot pay for."

(11) "I don't know about that. You've been in here and taken lunch more than once without drinking anything."

(12) "It may be so. I will make up for it now. Another glass, please."

(13) "First pay for what you have already drunk."

(14) "Frank, hand me your money," said Montagu.

(15) Frank incautiously handed him his small stock of money, which he saw instantly transferred to the bar-tender.

(16) "That is right, I believe," said Montagu Percy.

(17) The bar-keeper nodded, and Percy, transferring his attention to the free lunch, stowed away a large amount.

(18) Frank observed with some uneasiness the transfer of his entire cash capital to the bar-tender; but concluded that Mr. Percy would refund a part after they went out. As they reached the street he broached the subject.

(19) "I didn't agree to pay for both dinners," he said, uneasily.

(20) "Of course not. It will be my treat next time. That will be fair, won't it?"

(21) "But I would rather you would give me back a part of my money. I may not see you again."

(22) "I will be in the Park to-morrow at one o'clock."

(23) "Give me back ten cents, then," said Frank, uneasily. "That was all the money I had."

(24) "I am really sorry, but I haven't a penny about me. I'll make it right to-morrow. Good-day, my young friend. Be virtuous and you will be happy."

(25) Frank looked after the shabby figure ruefully. He felt that he had been taken in and done for. His small capital had vanished, and he was adrift in the streets of a strange city without a penny.

17. Why did Frank give Mr. Percy all his money?
   a. He was feeling generous
   b. Mr. Percy offered to pay for the sandwiches
   c. He owed it to Mr. Percy
   d. He thought Mr. Percy would give him some of it back

18. What does the phrase "his small capital" mean in paragraph 25?
   a. Frank's penny
   b. Frank's twenty-five cents
   c. Frank's virtuous nature
   d. Frank's friendship with Mr. Percy

19. Why did Frank agree to eat lunch?
   a. Mr. Percy was paying for it
   b. Lunch was completely free
   c. He only needed to buy a drink
   d. He wanted to spend time with Mr. Percy

20. Is Mr. Percy likely to pay Frank back?
   a. Yes, because he never orders what he cannot pay for
   b. Yes, because he will be in the Park the next day at one o'clock
   c. No, because Frank is not virtuous or happy
   d. No, because he's shown that he does not have any money

21. What adjective best describes Frank's feelings in paragraph 25?

    a. Disappointed
    b. Incautious
    c. Uneasy
    d. Suspicious

Questions 22 – 25 pertain to both "Andy Grant's Pluck" and "The Telegraph Boy passages":

22. How are Andy and Frank similar?

    a. They both have loving families
    b. They both have experienced misfortune
    c. They both were tricked
    d. They both need money for food

23. How are "Andy Grant's Pluck" and "The Telegraph Boy" different?

    a. "Andy Grant's Pluck" explains the circumstances that led to Andy's family misfortune, and "The Telegraph Boy" does not explain how Frank ended up with no money at all
    b. Andy is all alone, but Frank has many friends who can help him
    c. In "Andy Grant's Pluck," Andy is the victim of his family's bad luck but Frank in "The Telegraph Boy" is in trouble because he lost his own money
    d. "Andy Grant's Pluck" is about how Andy was tricked, and "The Telegraph Boy" is about how Frank lost his money

24. Both selections end with the main characters

    a. Feeling hopeful about the future
    b. Looking forward to going back to school
    c. In a dangerous situation
    d. Feeling uncertain about the future

25. Which of these sentences or phrases from "Andy Grant's Pluck" could also describe how Frank in the "The Telegraph Boy" feels at the end of the selection?

    a. He will receive no help from outside interest
    b. I must see how I can help father bear this burden
    c. Speaking with a cheerfulness which he did not feel
    d. We have met with misfortune

Questions 26 -31 pertain to the following passage:

The Great Round World and What is Going On In It by William Beverley Harison

(1) There is a new cause for supposing that the Treaty with Great Britain will either be defeated in the Senate, or else delayed for some time to come.

(2) This new trouble concerns the building of the Nicaragua Canal.

(3) It seems a remote cause, does it not? but it only shows how closely the affairs of one nation are bound up with those of all the others. No matter what our speech, our climate, or our color, we are all a portion of the great human family, and the good of one is the good of all.

(4) The Nicaragua Canal is a water-way that will cross the narrow neck of land that makes Central America. It will connect the Atlantic Ocean with the Pacific Ocean.

(5) With the help of such a canal, ships in going to the western coast of North or South America will not need to make the long and dangerous voyage around Cape Horn.

(6) Cape Horn, you will see if you look on your map, is the extreme southerly point of South America.

(7) There are so many storms and fogs there, that the Horn, as it is called, is much dreaded by sailors.

(8) Since the invention of steam, all the steamships go through the Straits of Magellan, and save the passage round the Horn; but there is not enough wind for sailing vessels in the rocky and narrow straits, so they still have to take the outside passage.

(9) The Straits of Magellan divide the main continent of South America from a group of islands, called Tierra del Fuego, and Cape Horn is the most southerly point of this archipelago.

(10) The journey down the coast of South America on the east, and up again on the west, takes such a long time, that the desire for a canal across the narrow neck of land which joins North and South America has been in men's minds for many years.

(11) A railway was built across the Isthmus of Panama to shorten the distance, and save taking the passage round the Horn. Travellers left their ship at one side of the Isthmus, and took the train over to the other, where they went on board another ship, which would take them the rest of their journey.

(12) This plan greatly increased the expense of the journey, and the canal was still so much wanted, that at last the Panama Canal was begun.

(13) You have all heard about the Panama Canal, which was to do the same work that the Nicaragua Canal is to do, that is, to connect the Atlantic and Pacific Oceans. You have probably heard how much time, labor, and human life was wasted over it, and how much trouble its failure caused in France.

(14) This Canal was to cut across the Isthmus at its very narrowest point. It was worked on for years, every one believing that it would be opened to ships before very long. Many of the maps and geographies that were printed in the eighties said that the Panama Canal would be opened in 1888, or at latest in 1889.

(15) No one expected what afterward happened. In 1889 the works were stopped for want of money; the affairs of the Canal were looked into; it was found that there had been dishonesty and fraud, and in 1892 the great Count Ferdinand de Lesseps, who built the Suez Canal, and a number of other prominent Frenchmen, were arrested for dealing dishonestly with the money subscribed for the Canal.

(16) There was a dreadful scandal; many of the high French officials had to give up their positions, and run away for fear of arrest.

(17) When the whole matter was understood, it was found that, for months before the work was stopped, the men who had charge of the Canal had decided that the work would cost such an enormous sum of money that it would be almost an impossibility to complete it.

(18) They did not have the honesty to let this be known, but allowed people to go on subscribing money, a part of which they put in their own pockets, and spent the rest in bribing the French newspapers not to tell the truth about the Canal.

(19) The worst of it was, that the money which had been subscribed was not from rich people, who would feel its loss very little, but from poor people, who put their savings, and the money they were storing away for their old age, into the Canal; and when they lost it, it meant misery and poverty to them.

(20) So the Panama Canal failed.

(21) But the project of making a canal was not given up. Two years before the idea of digging at Panama had been thought of, the ground where the Nicaragua Canal is being built had been surveyed, and thought better suited to the purpose than Panama.

(22) The reason for this was, that at Panama a long and deep cut had to be made through the mountains. This had to be done by blasting, in much the same way that the rocks are cleared away to build houses. This is a long and tedious work.

(23) The Nicaragua Canal will be 159 miles long, while the Panama, if it is ever completed, will be only 59 miles; but of these 159 miles, 117 are through the Nicaragua Lake and the San Juan River—water-ways already made by nature. For the remaining distance, there are other river-beds that will be used, and only 21 miles will actually have to be cut through.

(24) The main objection to this route for the Canal is, that there is a volcano on an island in the Nicaragua Lake, and there are always fears of eruptions and earthquakes in the neighborhood of volcanoes. A great eruption of the volcano might change the course of a river, or alter the face of the country so much, that the Canal might have to be largely remade.

26. The author mentions the treaty with Great Britain in paragraph 1 because people are concerned about

    a. A canal through Cape Horn
    b. The new Panama Canal
    c. The building of the Nicaragua Canal
    d. The Central America Canal

27. What are paragraphs 15-19 mostly about?

    a. The building of the Suez Canal
    b. The financial problems that ended the Panama Canal project
    c. The French newspapers, which did not tell the truth about the canal
    d. Ferdinand de Lesseps' experience in jail

28. Which sentence best shows the purpose for building the Nicaragua Canal?
    a. The new trouble concerns the building of the Nicaragua Canal
    b. Cape Horn, you will see if you look on your map, is the extreme southerly point of South America
    c. There are so many storms and fogs there, that the Horn, as it is called, is much dreaded by sailors
    d. Since the invention of steam, all the steamships go through the Straits of Magellan

29. What is the tone of this passage?
    a. Informational
    b. Humorous
    c. Mysterious
    d. Angry

30. Why will the Nicaragua Canal be easier to build than the Panama Canal?
    a. It is 100 miles longer than the Panama Canal
    b. It needs to be blasted through the mountains
    c. The San Juan River is already a complete canal
    d. Most of the canal will go through existing waterways

31. Look at the time line below.

Canals Around the World

According to the passage, what is the correct order of the time line?
    a. No change
    b. 1, 3, 2
    c. 2, 1, 3
    d. 3, 1, 2

32. The author probably wrote this selection to

a. Argue against the building of the Nicaragua Canal
b. Argue for the building of the Nicaragua Canal
c. Explain the problems that ended the Panama Canal project
d. Discuss new plans for a canal

33. Which words in paragraph 22 help the reader know what blasting means?

a. Long and deep cut
b. Had to be made
c. To build houses
d. Long and tedious work

34. What is the main problem in building the Nicaragua Canal?

a. Many of the financial backers, like Ferdinand de Lesseps, are in jail
b. The route needs to be cut through mountains
c. The Nicaragua Canal is interrupting the treaty with Great Britain
d. The canal route goes past a volcano

35. Why does the author discuss the Panama Canal?

a. He is highlighting the other great canal in Central America
b. He is explaining the reasons why a canal is needed
c. He is showing the first canal that was attempted and why it failed
d. He is explaining how sailors avoid going around Cape Horn

36. Read this phrase from paragraph 19: And when they lost it, it meant misery and poverty to them. The author uses this sentence to show:

a. The people who suffered the most from the failure to build the Panama Canal
b. Why the Panama Canal failed
c. Rich people suffered the most from the failure to build the Panama Canal
d. The project of making a canal was not given up

37. The Nicaragua Canal will?

a. Make sailing longer and more dangerous
b. Help ships avoid Cape Horn
c. Cause more people to take the train across the Isthmus of Panama
d. Cut across the Isthmus at its very narrowest point

Questions 38 – 48 pertain to the following passages:

"The Ettrick Shepherd" by James Baldwin

Part I

(1) In Scotland there once lived a poor shepherd whose name was James Hogg. His father and grandfather and great-grandfather had all been shepherds.

(2) It was his business to take care of the sheep which belonged to a rich landholder by the Ettrick Water. Sometimes he had several hundreds of lambs to look after. He drove these to the pastures on the hills and watched them day after day while they fed on the short green grass.

(3) He had a dog which he called Sirrah. This dog helped him watch the sheep. He would drive them from place to place as his master wished. Sometimes he would take care of the whole flock while the shepherd was resting or eating his dinner.

(4) One dark night James Hogg was on the hilltop with a flock of seven hundred lambs. Sirrah was with him. Suddenly a storm came up. There was thunder and lightning; the wind blew hard; the rain poured.

(5) The poor lambs were frightened. The shepherd and his dog could not keep them together. Some of them ran towards the east, some towards the west, and some towards the south.

(6) The shepherd soon lost sight of them in the darkness. With his lighted lantern in his hand, he went up and down the rough hills calling for his lambs.

(7) Two or three other shepherds joined him in the search. All night long they sought for the lambs.

(8) Morning came and still they sought. They looked, as they thought, in every place where the lambs might have taken shelter.

(9) At last James Hogg said, "It's of no use; all we can do is to go home and tell the master that we have lost his whole flock."

(10) They had walked a mile or two towards home, when they came to the edge of a narrow and deep ravine. They looked down, and at the bottom they saw some lambs huddled together among the rocks. And there was Sirrah standing guard over them and looking all around for help. "These must be the lambs that rushed off towards the south," said James Hogg.

(11) The men hurried down and soon saw that the flock was a large one.

(12) "I really believe they are all here," said one.

(13) They counted them and were surprised to find that not one lamb of the great flock of seven hundred was missing.

(14) How had Sirrah managed to get the three scattered divisions together? How had he managed to drive all the frightened little animals into this place of safety?

(15) Nobody could answer these questions. But there was no shepherd in

Scotland that could have done better than Sirrah did that night.

(16) Long afterward James Hogg said, "I never felt so grateful to any creature below the sun as I did to Sirrah that morning."

Part II

(17) When James Hogg was a boy, his parents were too poor to send him to school. By some means, however, he learned to read; and after that he loved nothing so much as a good book.

(18) There were no libraries near him, and it was hard for him to get books. But he was anxious to learn. Whenever he could buy or borrow a volume of prose or verse he carried it with him until he had read it through. While watching his flocks, he spent much of his time in reading. He loved poetry and soon began to write poems of his own. These poems were read and admired by many people.

(19) The name of James Hogg became known all over Scotland. He was often called the Ettrick Shepherd, because he was the keeper of sheep near the Ettrick Water.

(20) Many of his poems are still read and loved by children as well as by grown up men and women. Here is one:

A Boy's Song

Where the pools are bright and deep,

Where the gray trout lies asleep,

Up the river and o'er the lea,

That's the way for Billy and me.

Where the blackbird sings the latest,

Where the hawthorn blooms the sweetest,

Where the nestlings chirp and flee,

That's the way for Billy and me.

Where the mowers mow the cleanest,

Where the hay lies thick and greenest,

There to trace the homeward bee,

That's the way for Billy and me.

Where the hazel bank is steepest,

Where the shadow falls the deepest,

Where the clustering nuts fall free,

That's the way for Billy and me.

Why the boys should drive away,

Little maidens from their play,

Or love to banter and fight so well,

That's the thing I never could tell.

But this I know, I love to play

In the meadow, among the hay—

Up the water, and o'er the lea,

That's the way for Billy and me.

38. Why is James Hogg called the Ettrick Shepherd?
   a. He lived in Scotland
   b. He kept sheep
   c. He lived near Ettrick Water
   d. He lived near Ettrick Water and kept sheep

39. Which of the following best describes the problem in paragraphs 1-16?
   a. The sheep ran away and James Hogg couldn't find them
   b. A storm came up and Sirrah got scared
   c. James Hogg had trouble of taking care of such a large flock
   d. James Hogg got lost in the darkness

40. What does the phrase, Where the blackbird sings the latest, from the poem "A Boy's Song" refer to?
   a. James and Billy's favorite type of bird
   b. A place where James and Billy like to play
   c. The hay
   d. James and Billy's favorite song

41. In paragraphs 11-16, how does James know all the sheep were in the ravine?
   a. Sirrah told him
   b. He counted the sheep
   c. He rounded them all up from the east, the west, and the south
   d. He was the best shepherd in Scotland

42. What does the poem show about the narrator's personality?
   a. He is playful
   b. He is afraid of shadows
   c. He is not curious
   d. He does not like to explore things

43. Use the story map to answer the question below.

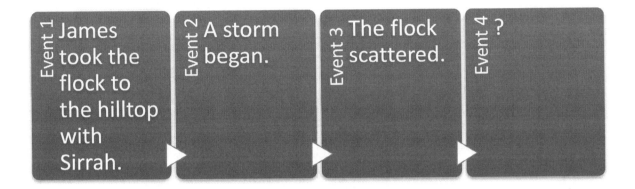

Which of these belongs in the empty box on the story map?

 a. James wrote a poem about his sheep
 b. James searched for the flock
 c. James lived in Scotland
 d. Sirrah gathered up all of the sheep

44. Why did James Hogg take care of the sheep?
 a. He took care of them as a favor to the landholder
 b. He loved the lambs
 c. Taking care of the sheep was his job
 d. He liked spending time with Sirrah

45. In paragraph 18, the word prose means
 a. Book
 b. Writing
 c. Library
 d. To learn

46. What's the most important idea is expressed in "A Boy's Song"?
 a. Billy and the narrator are great friends
 b. Being a shepherd is hard work
 c. The narrator enjoys nature
 d. Billy and the narrator fight frequently

47. In paragraph 8, the word sought means?
   a. To see
   b. To think
   c. To seek
   d. to come

48. Which word best describes how James felt after he located the sheep?
   a. Surprised
   b. Scared
   c. Tired
   d. Disappointed

Written Expression

Having the ability to write well will serve you well throughout your entire life, so it's an important skill to cultivate. There are many different elements that go into writing well. Some of them, such as spelling, punctuation, and capitalization, are covered more in depth in other parts of this guide. In this section, you'll be focusing on sentence structure, effective language, and clarity. All of these are components of good writing. When you master them, you'll be able to clearly and easily communicate with others in written form, without having to worry about being misunderstood. These exercises will help you improve in this area.

Questions 1 – 12 pertain to the following passage:

Mammie

(1) Characters:

ANTHONY – The young husband

MANDIE – The young wife

MAMMIE – Anthony's mother

(2) Setting:

Mammie's kitchen; the appliances are old, and a farmhouse table dominates the small room.

(3) The scene opens with Mandie clinging to Anthony. They are alone in the kitchen.

(4) MANDIE: Please don't leave me here with… her. She doesn't like me.

(5) ANTHONY: Of course she likes you. Don't be silly. Why wouldn't she like you?

(6) MANDIE: Oh, I don't know. She just doesn't. You don't know how she can be.

(7) ANTHONY: Don't I? I only lived with her for the first twenty years of my life.

(8) MANDIE: (pleading) Anthony, you can't go. Just take me with you. We can come back for dinner, just like you promised Mammie.

(9) ANTHONY: (taking Mandie firmly by the shoulders) No, Mandie. You're here, and you're staying. I'll only be gone for an hour or two. I promise to be back for dinner.

(10) MANDIE: But, Anthony—

(11) ANTHONY: Shush! She'll hear you—Mammie!

(12) Mammie enters, straightening her apron. She looks Mandie up and down. Anthony moves to kiss Mammie's cheek and Mandie reluctantly does the same.

(13) MAMMIE: Hello, Anthony. Hello, Amanda.

(14) ANTHONY: Well, Mammie, I'm afraid it's hello and goodbye for me. I'm off to my meeting. (He kisses Mandie.) You two girls have fun. I'll be back for dinner.

(15) Anthony exits. Mandie and Mammie look at each other for several seconds. The silence becomes uncomfortable. Finally, Mammie turns her back on Mandie and begins preparing dinner. She takes pots, pans, and ingredients out of the cupboards.

(16) MANDIE: (clearing her throat) So, um, what are you making for dinner?

(17) MAMMIE: (without turning around) Baked chicken. Rice. Asparagus.

(18) MANDIE: Oh. (Pauses) Could I help with something?

(19) Mammie wordlessly takes out a large pot and a bag of rice. She hands the items to Mandie and turns back to her work.

(20) MAMMIE: You can make the rice.

(21) Mandie stands very still, holding the rice and the pot. She bites her lip. She looks very frightened. Finally, Mammie turns around to face Mandie.

(22) MAMMIE: Well, child? What is it?

(23) MANDIE: (looking at the floor) I-I don't know how to make rice.

(24) MAMMIE: Don't know how to make rice? Don't be silly. Everyone knows how to make rice.

(25) MANDIE: (starting to cry) Everyone... except... me!

(26) Mammie sighs and wipes her hands on her apron. She comes over and takes the pot and the rice away from Mandie. She sets them on the table and gently chucks Mandie under the chin.

(27) MAMMIE: Come, child. It's nothing to cry over. Hush now. What can you cook?

(28) MANDIE: (sniffling) I can make brownies, I guess.

(29) MAMMIE: Good. (Patting Mandie awkwardly on the shoulder) Get to work, then.

(30) Mandie starts opening cupboard doors and pulling out ingredients. Mammie hands her a mixing bowl and measuring cups.

(31) MANDIE: Thank you.

(32) They work in silence for a while. After Mammie puts the chicken in the oven and puts the rice on to cook, she turns and watches Mandie work. Her face softens.

(33) MAMMIE: I suppose it's just as well, you know. Anthony always did like brownies better than rice. (She smiles and sits at the table.) I remember that when he was little, he always used to stick his finger into the middle brownie as soon as I took the pan from the oven. He always burned himself something terrible, but he couldn't let anyone else have that soft, gooey center brownie.

(34) MANDIE: (giggling) He still does that.

(35) MAMMIE: (shocked) No! A big, grown man like Anthony?

(36) MANDIE: Every time I make a batch of brownies.

(37) Mandie pours the batter into a brownie pan. Mammie watches her intently.

(38) MAMMIE: (motioning to the chair beside her) Come, child. Have a seat. Tell me more about my Anthony.

(39) Mandie sits and they chat for a while. Anthony reenters and looks surprised to see them sitting together.

(40) ANTHONY: (kissing Mandie) Hello, ladies. Something smells good. (He looks around.) And is that a pan of brownies waiting to go into the oven?

(41) MANDIE: Yes, Anthony. Now, go make yourself comfortable in the living room. We'll call you for dinner.

(42) ANTHONY: (bewildered) Well, okay... I guess. Are you sure you don't want me to stay in here?

(43) MANDIE: I'm sure. We have work to do. Now, go on.

(44) Anthony leaves, shaking his head and muttering to himself.

(45) MAMMIE: Besides, we can't talk about him when he's here!

(46) They both laugh and move to finish the dinner preparations, chatting amiably.

1. Which of the following is the best definition of the word "dominates" as it is used in paragraph 2?
- a. Diminishes
- b. Takes over
- c. Destroys
- d. Bosses around

2. How would you describe Mandie's feelings at the beginning of the play in relation to being left alone with Mammie?
- a. Desperate
- b. Excited
- c. Depressed
- d. Contented

3. Which paragraph best depicts Anthony's dismissive attitude toward Mandie's concerns?
- a. Paragraph 2
- b. Paragraph 3
- c. Paragraph 5
- d. Paragraph 7

4. Based on the information presented in the play, who is Mammie to Anthony?
- a. His aunt
- b. His grandmother
- c. His cousin
- d. His mother

5. How does the use of action and silence in this play contribute to the development of Mammie's character?
   a. It does not contribute to the development of Mammie's character
   b. It shows she is a poor communicator
   c. It demonstrates the awkwardness of her relationship with Mandie
   d. It shows her love for Anthony

6. Which paragraph best demonstrates Mammie's critical tendencies?
   a. Paragraph 17
   b. Paragraph 20
   c. Paragraph 22
   d. Paragraph 24

7. Which paragraph best indicates Mandie's feelings about Mammie?
   a. Paragraph 3
   b. Paragraph 4
   c. Paragraph 8
   d. Paragraph 10

8. What experience do Mandie and Mammie have in common that opens the door for them to bond with each other?
   a. Anthony hates both of their cooking
   b. Their rice always ends up overdone
   c. Anthony sticks his finger into both their brownie batches
   d. They both know how to bake brownies

9. What is the author's main purpose in writing this play?
   a. To show that shared experiences provide relational connections
   b. To emphasize the importance of getting along as a family
   c. To highlight the detriments of familial disharmony
   d. To exhibit a "slice of life" view of everyday Americana

10. Which of the following is a minor detail in this play?
   a. Mammie is Mandie's mother-in-law
   b. Mandie is afraid of Mammie
   c. Anthony is leaving Mandie alone with Mammie for a while
   d. Mandie knows how to make brownies

11. Which of the following is a critique, rather than a summary of this play?
   a. This play examines the dynamics between a young wife and her mother-in-law
   b. This play is a powerful, poignant look at the importance of communication
   c. This play shows how common experiences can help build relationships
   d. This play offers a look at the relationships of a man, his mother, and his wife

12. Which word in paragraph 43 best illustrates the newfound camaraderie between Mandie and Mammie?

a. We
b. Sure
c. Go
d. Work

Questions 13 – 24 pertain to the following passage:

Vegetarian Victory

(1) I remember the day I came home and told my mom I was planning on becoming a vegetarian. It was the summer before my junior year of high school, and Mom just nodded and smiled knowingly. She assumed it was another phase, like my short-lived hot pink mohawk, or the now-passé pegged jeans. But it wasn't a phase. For the past decade, I have lived a vegetarian lifestyle because it is healthy, wallet-friendly, and environmentally wise.

(2) Most people are familiar with at least some of the health benefits of a vegetarian lifestyle. But many people also believe that sacrificing meat means sacrificing taste. Not true. I can easily get my required 50 grams of protein each day through beans, nuts, and seeds in dishes that are bursting with beautiful tastes. I use herbs and spices to make my food fun and flavorful. Best of all, by using plants to provide protein and punch in my diet I forego much of the fat and cholesterol that is so prevalent in animal products.

(3) By foregoing that fat and cholesterol, I also protect myself from a variety of common diseases and health conditions. Studies have shown, for example, that a vegetarian lifestyle reduces the risk of a variety of cancers and can even lower the incidence of Alzheimer's disease. In addition, a vegetarian lifestyle has been shown to improve digestion, lower blood pressure and cholesterol levels, and protect against type II diabetes. In essence, I consider vegetables my super-weapon in the war against weariness!

(4) While the vegetarian lifestyle is clearly beneficial to my health, it also boosts my finances. Many people believe vegetarian foods—including fresh fruits and vegetables and alternative protein sources like soy—are just too expensive. To a certain extent, that may be true. But while the foods I eat may cost more than processed, packaged junk, my reward is fewer trips to the doctor and dentist. With the reduced incidence of disease comes a reduced need for treatments and medications. In the long run, the savings on medical costs more than makes up for the price of healthy food.

(5) The cost savings do not end with medical costs, however. I also save the money I used to spend on fast food and vending machines. My first two years of high school, I was a junk-food junkie. If you could get it at the drive-through or from a machine, I ate it. But after a while, all that junk made a sizeable dent in my wallet. When I became a vegetarian, I noticed that my cravings began to change. It didn't happen overnight, but over time I no longer craved the oily, greasy, and fatty food that drained my energy and my savings account. In fact, those types of foods actually started to make

me sick. Now, I walk with a granola bar or tin of almonds in my pocket for convenient snacking. I'm saving my money and my health, all at once.

(6) Not only does my vegetarian lifestyle save my money and my health, it also helps save the environment. By choosing plant proteins over animal products, I am saving the lives of countless animals in my lifetime. I don't have to lie awake at night wondering about slaughterhouse horrors or inhumane living conditions. Whether or not all the stories of such things are true, I don't obsess about contributing to that industry anymore. More animals, raised more naturally, create a better prospect and future for our world.

(7) Many people do not realize that the livestock industry—run primarily for food consumption—is one of the largest contributors of greenhouse gases in our environment. Thousands of cattle milling about in dusty feed lots, long treks from farm to marketplace in large trucks, and other factors add up to a huge environmental impact. By choosing a vegetarian lifestyle, I reduce the demand for this industry, thereby reducing their level of production and both their carbon footprint and mine. My personal choice might not change the world, but I can do my best to change my corner of the community.

(8) Becoming a vegetarian is a very personal choice. I chose this lifestyle because it benefits my overall health and protects me from certain disease processes. I also chose this lifestyle because it benefits my finances by reducing my expenditures for health care and junk food. Finally, I chose this lifestyle because it benefits the environment, reducing the demands on the livestock industry and shrinking my carbon footprint. I know this choice works for me, but I never pressure my friends to become vegetarians. I tell them my story with pride, but I understand they must make the choice for themselves, and vegetarianism is not for everyone. Still, I never know when I might inspire someone else to have a vegetarian victory—just like mine!

13. Which of the following words is the best synonym for "passé" as it is used in paragraph 1?
   a. Outdated
   b. Fashionable
   c. Foolish
   d. Memorable

14. What are the three key benefits of a vegetarian lifestyle listed in this article?
   a. Health benefits, social benefits, environmental benefits
   b. Social benefits, financial benefits, environmental benefits
   c. Health benefits, financial benefits, social benefits
   d. Health benefits, financial benefits, environmental benefits

15. How long does the article say the author has been living a vegetarian lifestyle?
   a. 5 years
   b. 10 years
   c. 15 years
   d. The article does not give this information

16. **What does the author compare the vegetarian lifestyle to in paragraph 3?**

 a. A cancer
 b. A war
 c. A disease
 d. A weapon

17. **What point of view was used to write this article?**

 a. First person
 b. Second person
 c. Third person
 d. All of the above

18. **Which of the following best describes the author's perspective in this article?**

 a. The vegetarian lifestyle is the only way to go
 b. The vegetarian lifestyle doesn't work for most people
 c. The vegetarian lifestyle offers many benefits
 d. The vegetarian lifestyle is best lived short-term

19. **According to the article, how many grams of protein does the author need each day?**

 a. 35
 b. 45
 c. 50
 d. 10

20. **What does paragraph 1 mean when it says, "Mom just nodded and smiled knowingly"?**

 a. Mom was, by nature, a very wise, happy person
 b. Mom thought vegetarianism was just another phase
 c. Mom was a vegetarian and was happy her child was too
 d. Mom wasn't really listening because she was distracted

21. **Which of the following is a controlling idea in this article?**

 a. Beans, nuts, and seeds can provide protein
 b. The vegetarian lifestyle can improve finances
 c. The vegetarian lifestyle can reduce cholesterol
 d. Some slaughterhouses have inhumane conditions

22. **Which of the following is a critique of this article, rather than a summary?**

 a. This article clearly outlines the benefits of a vegetarian lifestyle
 b. This article is a persuasive piece about vegetarianism
 c. This article uses opinions to guilt people into vegetarianism
 d. This article urges people to consider a vegetarian lifestyle

23. **Which of the following represents the author's main objective in writing this article?**

 a. To open readers' eyes to the benefits of vegetarianism
 b. To force people to adopt a vegetarian lifestyle
 c. To clearly demonstrate the evils of eating animal products
 d. To illustrate the environmental impact of the livestock industry

24. Which paragraph best encapsulates the main ideas and purpose of this entire article?
 a. Paragraph 1
 b. Paragraph 3
 c. Paragraph 7
 d. Paragraph 8

Questions 25 – 29 pertain to the following short story:

Puck

(1) It was the second week of an unseasonably cool July. The sun had finally made a rare weekend appearance, and the suburban neighborhood sizzled with possibility. As the day slipped lazily into evening, sun-baked residents trickled back to their homes from the lakeshore and the park and the community pool. The air smelled of sunscreen, charcoal smoke, sweat, overcooked meat.

(2) Will Jensen tossed a football across the yard to his best friend, Troy Coons. Dusk was settling around them, but the thought of retreating to the confines of the house seemed sacrilegious.

(3) "Can you believe we're going to college in a few weeks?" Troy asked, lobbing the ball back to Will.

(4) "What I can't believe is that you and I will be six hundred miles apart," Will said, catching the ball easily. "I don't think we've gone more than three days without seeing each other since kindergarten."

(5) "Except for when you had chicken pox," Troy said. "And the time I went to Hawaii with my grandparents. Remember how we begged them to let you come in my luggage?"

(6) Will laughed and tossed the ball back. "Those things don't count," he argued.

(7) The ball went sideways and Troy lunged for it, tripping over a ragged little terrier lounging lazily on the lawn. Troy collapsed in a tangled heap and the ball bounced down, just beyond his outstretched hand.

(8) "Puck!" Troy groaned. "No dogs on the field!"

(9) Will sauntered over and scooped up the little dog. He plopped down onto the crisp brown grass and laughed at Troy. Will reached over and rolled the ball toward Troy.

(10) "Don't blame Puck for your clumsiness," Will said, idly scratching the dog's fuzzy scalp. "How was he supposed to know you'd come stumbling through his daydreams?"

(11) Troy chuckled. Then they sat in silence as darkness swirled around them. Light glowed from windows thrown hopefully open to the faint breeze. Above them, the stars winked on in the charcoal sky. In the distance, leftover fireworks crackled and fizzed. The night was ripe with memories to be made.

(12) "Are you taking Puck with you?" Troy finally asked, breaking the silence.

(13) "Nah. No dogs in the dorm. Besides, Puck would hate being locked up in a room. He's spent the last sixteen years being king of the castle. He'll be happier here. That way he can greet me whenever I make it back home."

(14) Will lifted Puck and held him in mid-air. Puck wriggled playfully and licked Will's nose with his doughy pink tongue. Will laughed and set him down.

(15) "I sure will miss him, though," Will said, wiping Puck's saliva from his nose. "Puck's been a part of every memory I've had since I was really little."

(16) Troy faked a sniffle. "Stop, man. Just stop. I'm tearing up over here."

(17) Will punched Troy's arm good-naturedly. "Shut up!"

(18) A low, loud car careened around the corner, shattering the stupor of the summer night. Puck ran barking toward the car as it wove across the street like a wayward pinball.

(19) Seized with sudden panic, Will scrambled to his feet. "Puck, no! Come back!"

(20) As Will reached the sidewalk, Puck darted into the street. In a terrible, slow-motion montage, Will heard the tires squeal and Puck's bark turn to a startled yelp. Then the car sped away, and silence smothered the chaos.

(21) Will ran into the street. People peeked from doorways and windows, searching for the source of the commotion. Will fell beside Puck's limp body. Puck whimpered quietly and struggled to lick Will's hand. Then he was still.

(22) "No, Puck! No!" Will screamed. Shock rang in his ears and he was dizzy with emotion. Troy put a hand on Will's shoulder, but Will shook it off. He didn't want to be comforted. He wanted to wallow and writhe in the pool of pain that was slowly spreading through his soul.

(23) Every memory he had with Puck flooded his mind. This was not how it was supposed to be. Puck was supposed to be waiting for him when he came home from college. He was supposed to watch at the window as Will drove away and be there wagging with excitement whenever Will came home. He was supposed to be the constant in Will's changing life. This was not part of the plan.

(24) Will stayed in the road for a long time, crouched over Puck's familiar, lifeless body. He felt numb, empty, and emotionless. Finally, Will's mother led him gently from the street. Troy and Will's father gathered Puck's body carefully into a sheet. Neighbors watched in sympathy as the sorrowful party crossed the lawn.

(25) They walked in silence as darkness swirled around them. Lights still glowed from windows thrown hopefully open to the faint breeze. Above them, stars still winked on in the charcoal sky. In the distance, leftover fireworks still crackled and fizzed. Everything was the same, and nothing was the same. Puck was gone. And Will knew things would never really be the same again.

25. In paragraph 2, what does "sacrilegious" mean?
   a. Absurdly inappropriate
   b. Nasty and evil
   c. A waste of time
   d. Holy and good

26. Which of the following best describes Will's attitude in paragraph 15?
   a. Angry
   b. Cheerful
   c. Sentimental
   d. Annoyed

27. What type of figurative language is used to describe the stars in paragraph 11?
   a. Simile
   b. Personification
   c. Metaphor
   d. Paradox

28. How is Puck's death an example of irony?
   a. Will was worried about missing Puck while Will was away at college, and now he will miss him forever
   b. Will wanted Puck to die so Will didn't have to think about him while he was away at college
   c. Puck was always quiet and docile, but he was strangely driven to run after that one car
   d. Troy hated Puck, and he wanted Puck to be hit by the passing car

29. Which of the following is a main idea in this story?
   a. The passing car is playing loud music
   b. Troy misses the ball when he trips over Puck
   c. Will and Troy like to play football
   d. Will has had Puck for a very long time

Questions 30 – 34 pertain to the following short story:

What I Will Always Remember

(1) I will always remember my grandfather, wiry and strong, hoisting me onto his shoulders as he showed me around the rail yard where he worked. His shock of shiny black hair glistened in the sunlight, flanked by silvery sideburns. High atop his shoulder, I owned the world. Everyone looked up to me, but I looked up to him. We played together like wayward children. He was larger than life, and I was proud he was my grandfather.

(2) I will always remember my grandfather, tainted with the first pangs of age, standing and proudly applauding at my high school graduation. He was grayer and weaker, but still robust. We stood eye to eye, but I still looked up to him. I craved his wisdom, his patience, his guidance. We talked together like two best pals. He was still larger than life, and I was proud he was my grandfather.

(3) I will always remember my grandfather, wrapped in the first throes of Parkinson's disease, watching me receive my college degree. He was paler and thinner and too weak to stand, but he applauded boisterously when my name was called. I towered above his wheelchair, but I still looked up to him. I needed his support, his affirmation, his

companionship. We sat together like two old friends. He was still larger than life, and I was proud he was my grandfather.

(4) I will always remember my grandfather, lost in the last weeks of his life, sitting quietly with me on the front porch. His skin was translucent with the pallor of death, and his body was wracked by endless tremors. I fed him with a syringe, gently coaxing the food down his throat. He was shrunken and powerless, but I still looked up to him. We clung to our memories together like two sailors lost at sea. He was still larger than life, and I was proud he was my grandfather.

(5) Today I remembered my grandfather, cocooned in his flag-draped coffin as they lowered him into the ground. He was surrounded by those he had impacted in life. Today we honored a soldier, a worker, a teacher, a friend. We honored a husband, a father, a mentor, a guide. He was strong, even in weakness. He was wise, even in silence. He gave me everything, even when he had nothing to give, and I looked up to him. He will always be larger than life to me, and I will always be proud he was my grandfather.

30. In paragraph 4, what does "pallor" mean?

a. Brightness
b. Paleness
c. Jaundice
d. Darkness

31. How would you properly classify this piece of writing?

a. Informational essay
b. Fiction
c. Persuasive essay
d. Memoir

32. What is the author's main purpose in writing this piece?

a. To honor and say goodbye to Grandfather
b. To illustrate the ravages of age
c. To show the effects of Parkinson's disease
d. To chronicle Grandfather's life

33. What technique is used throughout this piece to increase its power and impact?

a. Plotting
b. Dialogue
c. Repetition
d. Citation

34. In paragraph 4, what image best illustrates Grandfather's powerlessness?

a. Sitting quietly on the porch
b. Being wracked with tremors
c. Being fed with a syringe
d. Having translucent skin

Questions 35 – 38 pertain to both short stories "Puck" and "What I Will Always Remember":

35. What theme do these two passages have most in common?
a. Loss of a loved one
b. The silence of summer
c. Companionship
d. Grandparents and friends

36. What is the difference in point of view between these two stories?
a. There is no difference in point of view between these two stories
b. One is written in third person and the other is written in first person
c. One is written in second person and the other is written in third person
d. One is written in first person and the other is written in second person

37. Why does the expression of grief seem more vivid in "Puck" than it does in "What I Will Always Remember"?
a. It does not seem more vivid in "Puck"
b. Will seems younger than the narrator in the other piece
c. The grief in "Puck" is more sudden and described in greater detail
d. Losing an animal is more painful than losing a grandparent

38. What is the primary similarity between paragraph 23 of "Puck" and paragraph 5 of "What I Will Always Remember"?
a. They both have seven sentences
b. They both express reminiscence in the face of loss
c. They are both centered on excessive emotion
d. They are both near the end of the piece

Questions 39 – 48 pertain to the following short story:

The Saga of "Sparky"

(1) Sparky was a loser, but he didn't stay that way. (2) You probably know Sparky better by his given name: Charles Schulz. (3) Nicknamed Sparky when he was a child, Charles schulz endured years of struggle before he finally found success. (4) Eventually, the loser became a winner. (5) Thanks to the hard work and perseverance of Sparky, the world will always remember a boy named Charlie Brown and the rest of the Peanuts gang.

(6) Sparky was born Charles Monroe Schulz on November 26, 1922, and he grew up in Minneapolis, Minnesota, where he struggled to fit in socially. (7) He skipped two grades, and as a result he struggled with his studies. (8) He was also painfully shy, so he never dated. (9) In addition, Sparky was inert at most sports. (10) But he loved to draw, drawing was his dream.

(11) Sparky poured his heart and soul into his drawings during his high school years. (12) He had a particular love for cartooning, and he unsuccessfully submitted several cartoons to his yearbook. (13) In the late 1940s, when Sparky was in his mid-twenties, his dream began to come true. (14) Although he was devastated when the cartoons were rejected by the yearbook committee, he remained determined to make

a living through his art someday. (15) He sold some cartoons to magazines and newspapers. (16) Someone finally appriciated his artistic ability.

(17) In 1950, Sparky created what would become his legacy; a comic called Peanuts. (18) The central character—Charlie Brown—was based on Sparky himself, and his lifelong struggle to fit in with the world around him. (19) Peanuts became an instant hit. (20) Adults and children alike were drawn to it because they could relate to the struggles of the characters.

(21) From its humble beginnings in the 1950s, Peanuts went on to become one of the most successful comics of all time. (22) Sparky lovingly hand-drew each of the 18,000 Peanuts comic strips, and they eventually appointed in over 2000 newspapers in more than 75 countries. (23) The Peanuts characters have appeared in comic strips, television specials, coloring books, children's books, and a variety of other media. (24) Although Sparky died in 2000, his work lives on. (25) His comics are still seen in dozens of newspapers each week. (26) Through hard work, perseverance, and believing in himself, Sparky turned his loser's lot into a story of success.

39. **Which of the following is the most appropriate correction for sentence 3?**
   a. Change Sparky to sparky
   b. Change Nicknamed to Nick-named
   c. Remove the comma after child
   d. Change Charles schulz to Charles Schulz

40. **Which sentence in paragraph 1 functions as the thesis statement for this composition?**
   a. Sentence 2
   b. Sentence 5
   c. Sentence 3
   d. Sentence 1

41. **In sentence 9, what change is necessary?**
   a. Change inert to inept
   b. Remove the comma after addition
   c. Change Sparky to sparky
   d. Change most to many

42. **What change, if any, should be made in sentence 10?**
   a. No change is necessary
   b. Remove the comma
   c. Replace the comma with a semicolon
   d. Replace the comma with a colon

43. **What change would most improve the organization of the third paragraph of this composition?**
   a. Swap sentences 13 and 14
   b. Move sentence 13 to the beginning of the paragraph
   c. Swap sentences 11 and 16
   d. Move sentence 12 to the end of the paragraph

44. What change, if any, should be made in sentence 16?

    a. No change is necessary
    b. Change finally to finaly
    c. Change appriciated to appreciated
    d. Change artistic to autistic

45. What change, if any, is needed in sentence 17?

    a. No change is necessary
    b. Replace the semicolon with a colon
    c. Replace the semicolon with a period
    d. Remove the semicolon

46. What punctuation change, if any, should be made in sentence 18?

    a. No change is necessary
    b. Remove the dashes
    c. Replace the second dash with a comma
    d. Replace the first dash with a colon

47. How does sentence 21 function as a transition between paragraph 4 and paragraph 5?

    a. Sentence 21 does not function as a transition
    b. It talks about a topic previously mentioned
    c. It demonstrates transition with the phrase "went on"
    d. It connects the history of Peanuts with the success of Sparky

48. In sentence 22, what word would be most appropriate to replace the misused word "appointed"?

    a. Approximated
    b. Appeared
    c. Appropriated
    d. Appositioned

Questions 49 – 58 pertain to the following essay:

The Very Best Season

(1) Ice cream cones shrink and drip in the stiffling heat. (2) Cool pools shimmer like a welcoming oasis. (3) The blazing sun hangs lazily for hours in the breathtakingly blue sky. (4) It's summer, and the whole world seems more content. (5) Summer is the very best season for three main reasons.

(6) First, Summer is the best season because school is out and the days are long and lazy. (7) Without structure and schedule, the nights were late and the afternoons roll on forever. (8) There is no homework, no pressure, and no deadlines. (9) There is no blaring alarm clock, just the endless cadence of birds and sprinklers and kids playing in the streets. (10) Everything feels more simpler and more relaxed.

(11) That sense of relaxation brings the second reason summer is the best season: the pace of life is slower. (12) No one seems to be in a hurry. (13) It is the season of hamocks and vacations and sandy seashores. (14) It is a time when the whole hectic, hurried world seems to pause and take a deep, cleansing breath. (15) The endless

42

Copyright © Mometrix Media. You have been licensed one copy of this document for personal use only. Any other reproduction or redistribution is strictly prohibited. All rights reserved.
This content is provided for test preparation purposes only and does not imply an endorsement by Mometrix of any particular political, scientific, or religious point of view.

days and hazy nights seem to add to the pleasant stupor. (16) All is calm, and all is bright.

(17) Despite the universal sense of relaxation summer is also the best season because there is so much to do. (18) Warm, dry weather lends itself perfectly to outdoor activities: camping in the cool, quiet woods; swimming in a crystal-clear stream; sunning on an emerald carpet of fragrant grass. (19) It is also the season of fairs, festivals, and farmers' markets. (20) There is never a shortage of fun.

(21) While every season of the year has its own unique charms, summer will always be the best season to me. (22) The long, lazy, school-free days are loved by me. (23) I love the slower, more relaxed pace of life. (24) Finally, I love the many fun activities that can fill the empty hours. (25) All of these things—and many more—make summer the very best season.

49. What change, if any, needs to be made in sentence 1?
a. No change is necessary
b. Change stiffling to stifling
c. Change cream to Cream
d. Insert a comma after shrink

50. Which sentence functions as the thesis statement for this essay?
a. Sentence 1
b. Sentence 4
c. Sentence 5
d. Sentence 10

51. In sentence 6, what correction, if any, is necessary?
a. No correction is necessary
b. Remove the comma after first
c. Insert a comma after season
d. Change Summer to summer

52. Which of the following is the best version of sentence 7?
a. Without structure and schedule, the nights are late and the afternoons roll on forever
b. Without structure and schedule, the nights are late and the afternoons rolled on forever
c. Without structure and schedule, the nights were late and the afternoons rolled on forever
d. The sentence is correct as it is written.

53. What correction, if any, is needed in sentence 10?
a. No correction is needed.
b. Change more simpler to simpler
c. Change feels to felt
d. Insert a comma after simpler

54. What change, if any, is needed in sentence 11?
a. No change is needed
b. Replace the colon with a semicolon
c. Replace the colon with a comma
d. Remove the colon

55. In sentence 13, what spelling error needs to be corrected?

a. Change season to session
b. Change hamocks to hammocks
c. Change seashores to seeshores
d. There is no spelling error in sentence 13

56. What change, if any, should be made in sentence 17?

a. No change is necessary.
b. Insert a comma after season
c. Insert a comma after Despite
d. Insert a comma after relaxation

57. What is the error in sentence 22?

a. It is a sentence fragment
b. It is a run-on sentence
c. It has passive construction
d. It has parallel structure

58. What correction, if any, needs to be made in sentence 25?

a. No correction is necessary
b. Remove the dashes
c. Replace the first dash with a colon
d. Replace the second dash with a comma

Mometrix

Mathematics

Acquiring math skills is one of the most important things you can do in life. That's why schools spend so much time on math instruction during your educational years. Of course, it's obvious that you'll need to have enough math proficiency to graduate from high school, but that's only the beginning.

No matter what you aspire to in life, or what career you're hoping to embark upon, you'll need math skills to help you reach your goals. The better you are at math, the better your chances of reaching your goals will be. This is especially true if you hope to become a professional, such as a doctor, lawyer, dentist, etc. You'll need excellent math abilities in order to get into and graduate from suitable college programs for these careers.

1. Which of the following is listed in order from *least to greatest*?

    a. $-2, -\frac{3}{4}, -0.45, 3\%, 0.36$

    b. $-\frac{3}{4}, -0.45, -2, 0.36, 3\%$

    c. $-0.45, -2, -\frac{3}{4}, 3\%, 0.36$

    d. $-2, -\frac{3}{4}, -0.45, 0.36, 3\%$

2. Which of the following is listed in order from greatest to least?

    a. $\frac{4}{5}, \frac{7}{8}, \frac{1}{2}, -8, -3$

    b. $\frac{7}{8}, \frac{4}{5}, \frac{1}{2}, -3, -8$

    c. $\frac{4}{5}, \frac{1}{2}, \frac{7}{8}, -3, -8$

    d. $\frac{7}{8}, \frac{4}{5}, \frac{1}{2}, -8, -3$

3. A pentagon with side lengths of 9 cm, 18 cm, 24 cm, 18 cm, and 9 cm is dilated by a scale factor of $\frac{1}{3}$. Which of the following represents the dimensions of the dilated pentagon?

    a. 3 cm, 9 cm, 8 cm, 9 cm, 3 cm

    b. 6 cm, 3 cm, 12 cm, 6 cm, 3 cm

    c. 3 cm, 6 cm, 8 cm, 6 cm, 3 cm

    d. 6 cm, 18 cm, 9 cm, 6 cm, 9 cm

4. Adrian measures the circumference of a circular picture frame, with a radius of 3 inches. Which of the following is the best estimate for the circumference of the frame?

    a. 12 inches

    b. 16 inches

    c. 18 inches

    d. 24 inches

5. Each week, a family orders one large pizza. The family eats approximately $\frac{5}{6}$ of each pizza. Which of the following best represents the number of whole pizzas the family eats in 5 weeks?

    a. 3

    b. 4

    c. 5

    d. 6

M@metrix

6. The cruising altitude of a plane on a particular trip is recorded as 2.71×10^4 feet. Which of the following represents the cruising altitude?

a. 2,710 feet
b. 27,100 feet
c. 207,100 feet
d. 271,000 feet

7. A fundraising group charges $0.25 per cookie and has a daily expense of $18. Which of the following describes the steps that need to be taken, in order to calculate the daily profit, when selling 49 cookies?

a. Multiply 49 by $0.25 and subtract $18
b. Multiply 49 by $0.25 and divide by $18
c. Multiply 49 by $0.25 and add $18
d. Multiply 49 by $18 and subtract $0.25

8. Kyle has $950 in savings and wishes to donate one-fifth of it to 8 local charities. He estimates that he will donate around $30 to each charity. Which of the following correctly describes the reasonableness of his estimate?

a. It is reasonable because $240 is one-fifth of $900
b. It is reasonable because $240 is less than one-fifth of $1,000
c. It is not reasonable because $240 is more than one-fifth of $1,000
d. It is not reasonable because $240 is one-fifth of $1,000

9. Martin's bed is 7 feet long. Which of the following represents the length of the bed, in centimeters?

a. 209.42 cm
b. 213.36 cm
c. 215.52 cm
d. 217.94 cm

10. A tube of lotion costs $4.85 and contains 7.3 ounces of lotion. Which of the following best represents the cost of 5 ounces of lotion?

a. $3.18
b. $3.24
c. $3.32
d. $3.48

11. Which of the following describes a proportional relationship?

a. Jonathan opens a savings account, with an initial deposit of $150, and deposits $125 per month
b. Bruce pays his employees $12 per hour worked, during the month of December, as well as a $250 bonus
c. Alvin pays $28 per month for his phone service, plus $0.07 for each long distance minute used
d. Kevin drives 65 miles per hour

12. The tables below represent the number of laptops sold per hour at four different electronic stores. Which store did *not* report a proportional relationship between number of hours and number of laptops sold?

a.

Number of Hours	Number of Laptops Sold
1	3
2	6
3	9
4	12

b.

Number of Hours	Number of Laptops Sold
1	6
2	12
3	18
4	24

c.

Number of Hours	Number of Laptops Sold
1	4
2	8
3	12
4	16

d.

Number of Hours	Number of Laptops Sold
1	7
2	11
3	15
4	19

13. Which of the following describes a graph that represents a proportional relationship?

    a. The graph has a slope of 2,500 and a y-intercept of 250
    b. The graph has a slope of 1,500 and a y-intercept of −150
    c. The graph has a slope of 2,000 and a y-intercept of 0
    d. The graph has a slope of −1,800 and a y-intercept of −100

14. Andy is offered a discount of 15% off of a vehicle, priced at $39,500. How much money will he save with the discount?

    a. $5,325
    b. $5,655
    c. $5,925
    d. $6,005

15. The perimeter of a building on an architectural drawing is 50 centimeters. If 2 centimeters represents 80 feet, what is the perimeter of the actual building?

    a. 2,000 feet
    b. 1,200 feet
    c. 900 feet
    d. 1,800 feet

16. Triangle DEF is similar to Triangle ABC. What is the length of $\overline{DF}$?

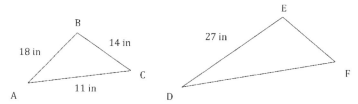

a. 18.5 in
b. 20 in
c. 16.5 in
d. 22 in

17. Which of the following graphs represents the linear relationship shown in the table below?

x	y
−3	−31
−1	−13
0	−4
1	5
3	23

a.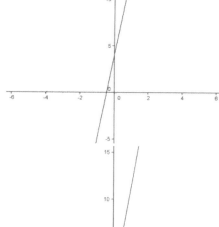

b.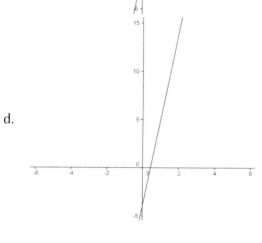

c.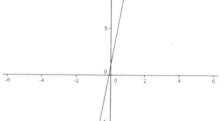

d.

18. Mia earns $2,500 per month, plus 5% of each insurance premium sold. Which of the following equations represents the amount of money she earns each month?
   a. $y = \frac{2500}{0.05x} + 2500$
   b. $y = 2500x + 0.05$
   c. $y = 2500.05x$
   d. $y = 0.05x + 2500$

19. Which of the following equations represents the values, shown in the table below?

x	y
-2	5
1	-4
3	-10
6	-19

   a. $y = -3x + 1$
   b. $y = -4x - 2$
   c. $y = -3x - 1$
   d. $y = -2x + 1$

20. Which equation is represented by the graph shown below?

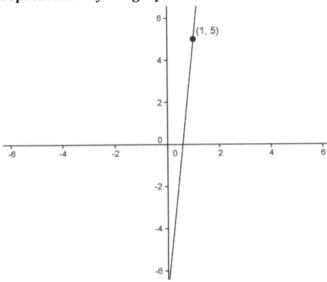

   a. $y = 12x - 7$
   b. $y = 14x - 7$
   c. $y = 8x - 7$
   d. $y = 10x - 7$

21. Hannah's parents open a savings account for her, with an initial deposit of $245. They deposit $125 per month into her account. Without considering interest earned, how much money will be in Hannah's account after 5 years?
   a. $11,205
   b. $9,805
   c. $7,745
   d. $14,825

22. What is the 46th term in a sequence, given by the equation, $y = 6x - 8$, where x represents the term number and y represents the value of the term?

    a. 256
    b. 262
    c. 268
    d. 274

23. Given the sequence: $-3, -8, -13, -18, ...$, what is the 21st term in the sequence?

    a. −98
    b. −103
    c. −108
    d. −113

24. A triangle has dimensions of 9 cm, 4 cm, and 7 cm. The triangle is reduced by a scale factor of $\frac{3}{4}$. Which of the following represents the dimensions of the dilated triangle?

    a. 8.25 cm, 3.25 cm, 6.25 cm
    b. 4.5 cm, 2 cm, 3.5 cm
    c. 6.75 cm, 3 cm, 5.25 cm
    d. 4.95 cm, 2.2 cm, 3.85 cm

25. A rectangle has a width of 9 inches and a length of 15 inches. If the rectangle is enlarged by a scale factor of $\frac{3}{2}$, what is the perimeter of the dilated rectangle?

    a. 68 inches
    b. 72 inches
    c. 60 inches
    d. 64 inches

26. Which of the following vertices represents the reflection of the triangle, shown below, about the x-axis?

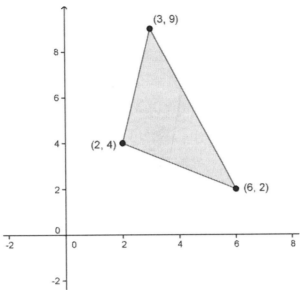

   a. (3, −9), (2, −4), (6, −2)
   b. (−3, −9), (−2, −4), (−6, −2)
   c. (9, 3), (4, 2), (2, 6)
   d. (−3, 9), (−2, 4), (−6, 2)

27. The trapezoid below is shifted 4 units up and 8 units to the left. Which of the following represents the vertices of the translated figure?

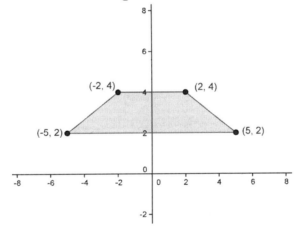

   a. (6, −13), (8, −10), (8, −6), (6, −3)
   b. (3, 6), (6, 8), (10, 8), (13, 6)
   c. (−13, −2), (−10, 4), (−6, 0), (−3, −2)
   d. (−13, 6), (−10, 8), (−6, 8), (−3, 6)

28. Triangle ABC has side lengths of 18 inches, 9 inches, and 11 inches. The triangle is enlarged by a scale factor of 4. Which of the following represents the side lengths of the enlarged triangle?

   a. 36 inches, 18 inches, 22 inches
   b. 72 inches, 36 inches, 44 inches
   c. 14 inches, 5 inches, 7 inches
   d. 36 inches, 27 inches, 44 inches

29. What is the name of the figure shown below?

   a. Triangular prism
   b. Triangular pyramid
   c. Square pyramid
   d. Rectangular prism

30. What is the ordered pair, represented by Point P, plotted on the graph below?

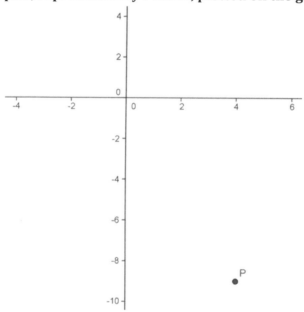

   a. (−4, −9)
   b. (−4, 9)
   c. (4, 9)
   d. (4, −9)

31. What is the name of the figure shown below?

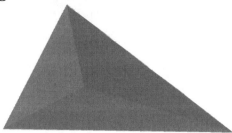

   a. Square pyramid
   b. Cube
   c. Triangular prism
   d. Triangular pyramid

32. If the two ends are congruent equilateral triangles, what is the lateral surface area of the figure shown below?

   a. 180 cm²
   b. 270 cm²
   c. 540 cm²
   d. 720 cm²

33. What is the surface area of the figure shown below?

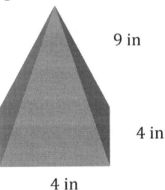

   a. 68 in²
   b. 88 in²
   c. 121 in²
   d. 144 in²

34. Amanda ships a box, with dimensions of 18 inches, 9 inches, and 6 inches. How many cubic inches of space does she have inside the box?

   a. 486
   b. 524
   c. 972
   d. 1022

35. Which of the following best represents the lateral surface area of the cylinder shown below?

r = 8 in

h = 14

   a. 351.68 in²
   b. 703.36 in²
   c. 904.72 in²
   d. 1,202.96 in²

36. Which of the following represents the formula for finding the volume of the figure shown below?

   a. $V = \frac{1}{3}\pi r^2 h$
   b. $V = \frac{1}{3}\pi r h$
   c. $V = \pi r^2 h$
   d. $V = 3\pi r^2 h$

37. Marcele purchases a television as a gift to her husband. She needs to wrap the box, containing the television. If the box has dimensions of 22 inches by 19 inches by 17 inches, how many square inches of wrapping paper will she need?

   a. 1,820
   b. 2,110
   c. 2,230
   d. 2,460

38. The figure below has a volume equal to the product of the area of the base and the height. Which of the following formulas represents the area of the base?

a. $A = \frac{1}{2}bh$
b. $A = bh$
c. $A = \frac{1}{3}bh$
d. $A = 2bh$

39. The figure below has a volume equal to the product of π and which other term?

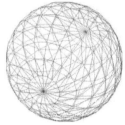

a. $\frac{4}{3}r^3$
b. $\frac{1}{3}r^2$
c. $\frac{1}{3}r^3$
d. $\frac{4}{3}r^2$

40. Brian designs a cylindrical container. He wishes to paint only the lateral face. If the cylinder has a radius of 6 inches and a height of 8 inches, how many square inches of the container will he paint?

a. 48π inches²
b. 96π inches²
c. 108π inches²
d. 144π inches²

41. Oliver wants to walk from his home to the park. The locations of his home, the park, and the school are shown on the diagram below. Which of the following best represents the distance from Oliver's home to the park, when walking the diagonal path?

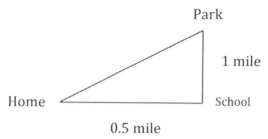

a. 0.6 mile
b. 0.8 mile
c. 1.1 mile
d. 1.4 mile

42. A right triangle has an area of 28 cm². Which of the following represents the possible measurements of the base and height of a similar right triangle?

a. 14 cm and 4 cm
b. 14 cm and 16 cm
c. 21 cm and 24 cm
d. 7 cm and 2 cm

43. The side lengths of a square are increased by a factor of 6. Which of the following correctly describes the effect on the area?

a. The area is increased by 36
b. The area is 12 times larger
c. The area is 36 times larger
d. The area is increased by 12

44. A cylinder has a height of 9 inches and a radius of 4 inches. If the height remains the same, but the radius increases by 8 inches, what is the effect on the volume of the cylinder?

a. It will be 7 times larger
b. It will be 9 times larger
c. It will increase by 3,548 cubic inches
d. It will increase by 3,576 cubic inches

45. Carmen flips a coin and draws a card from a deck. What is the probability she gets heads and draws an ace?

a. $\frac{15}{26}$
b. $\frac{4}{13}$
c. $\frac{1}{26}$
d. $\frac{2}{13}$

46. Eli rolls a die and flips a coin. What is the probability he rolls an even number or gets tails?

   a. $\dfrac{1}{4}$

   b. $\dfrac{1}{2}$

   c. $\dfrac{3}{4}$

   d. 1

47. Monique rolls a die and spins a spinner, with six equally spaced sections, labeled 1 – 6. What is the probability she rolls a number less than 4 or the spinner lands on 2?

   a. $\dfrac{1}{12}$

   b. $\dfrac{5}{8}$

   c. $\dfrac{1}{3}$

   d. $\dfrac{2}{3}$

48. Jasper rolls a die. What is the probability he rolls an even number or a number less than 5?

   a. $\dfrac{2}{3}$

   b. $\dfrac{5}{6}$

   c. $\dfrac{1}{3}$

   d. $\dfrac{1}{2}$

49. Johnson rolls a die 18 times. Which of the following is the best prediction for the number of times he will roll a number greater than 4?

   a. 3

   b. 6

   c. 9

   d. 12

50. The number of houses Amelia has sold per year over the past ten years is listed below:

     42, 36, 39, 45, 13, 47, 38, 41, 44, 34

Which of the following measures will most accurately reflect the number of houses she sold per year?

   a. Mean

   b. Median

   c. Mode

   d. Range

51. Gitta wishes to represent the median number of miles driven per month. Which representation will most directly reveal the median number of miles driven?

   a. Histogram

   b. Bar graph

   c. Stem-and-leaf plot

   d. Box-and-whisker plot

52. Yin wishes to track the number of new clients she has secured each year. Which of the following representations is most appropriate for displaying this data?

    a.   Line plot
    b.   Pie chart
    c.   Line graph
    d.   Stem-and-leaf plot

53. Which of the following is listed in order from least to greatest?

    a. $-\frac{3}{4}, -7\frac{4}{5}, -8, 18\%, 0.25, 2.5$
    b. $-8, -7\frac{4}{5}, -\frac{3}{4}, 0.25, 2.5, 18\%$
    c. $18\%, 0.25, -\frac{3}{4}, 2.5, -7\frac{4}{5}, -8$
    d. $-8, -7\frac{4}{5}, -\frac{3}{4}, 18\%, 0.25, 2.5$

54. Which of the following fractions is larger than $2\frac{1}{4}$ but smaller than $2\frac{2}{5}$?

    a. $2\frac{1}{2}$
    b. $2\frac{3}{8}$
    c. $2\frac{6}{11}$
    d. $2\frac{5}{9}$

55. Rectangle A is similar to Rectangle B. Rectangle A has a length of 18 cm and a width of 4 cm. If Rectangle B has a width of 6 cm, what is its length?

    a.   20 cm
    b.   24 cm
    c.   26 cm
    d.   27 cm

56. A carpenter builds a right triangular brace to support a cabinet corner. The brace must have a base of 9 inches and a height of 8 inches. Which of the following best represents the measurement of the hypotenuse of the brace?

    a.   12.02 inches
    b.   12.04 inches
    c.   12.06 inches
    d.   12.10 inches

57. A square has a perimeter of approximately 5.66 cm. Which of the following represents the area?

    a.   2 cm2
    b.   2.8 cm2
    c.   9.5 cm2
    d.   32 cm2

58. A cut board may not vary from the measurement specification by more than 0.0095 meters. Which of the following represents this amount, using scientific notation?

   a. 9.5×10^3 meters
   b. 9.5×10^{-2} meters
   c. 9.5×10^2 meters
   d. 9.5×10^{-3} meters

59. Pluto's distance from the sun is approximately 5.9×10^9 kilometers. Which of the following best represents this distance?

   a. 5,900,000
   b. 590,000,000
   c. 5,900,000,000
   d. 59,000,000,000

60. Each month, Aisha invests twice the amount invested the previous month. If she invested $26.25 during the first month, how much did she invest during the sixth month?

   a. $157.50
   b. $420.00
   c. $768.50
   d. $840.00

61. Jackson donates three dollars less than half the amount Amy donates. If Amy donates $128, how much does Jackson donate?

   a. $61
   b. $64
   c. $67
   d. $70

62. Lauren must travel a distance of 1,480 miles to get to her destination. She plans to drive approximately the same number of miles per day for 5 days. Which of the following is a reasonable estimate of the number of miles she will drive per day?

   a. 240 miles
   b. 260 miles
   c. 300 miles
   d. 340 miles

63. Adam builds a bridge that is 12 feet long. If 1 foot equals 0.3048 meters, which of the following best represents the length of the bridge, in meters?

   a. 1.83 meters
   b. 4.96 meters
   c. 3.66 meters
   d. 39.37 meters

64. Which of the following tables represents a proportional relationship?

a.

x	y
1	−3
2	2
3	7
4	12
5	17
6	22

b.

x	y
1	5
2	8
3	11
4	14
5	17
6	20

c.

x	y
1	6
2	12
3	18
4	24
5	30
6	36

d.

x	y
1	3
2	9
3	15
4	21
5	27
6	33

65. Which of the following linear equations represents a *non-proportional* relationship?

a. $y = 7x$

b. $y = \frac{x}{4}$

c. $y = \frac{1}{2}x$

d. $y = 2x + 8$

66. Eric's cumulative savings amount is entirely proportional to the number of months he has been saving. Which of the following graphs could represent this relationship?

a.
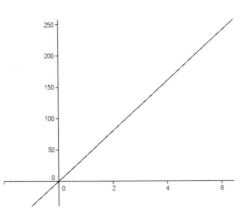

b.
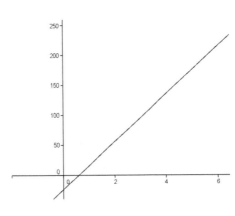

c.
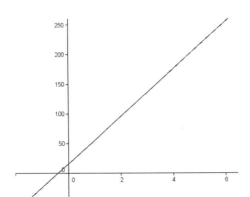

d.
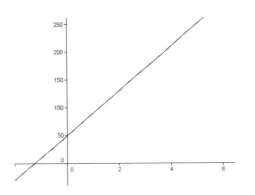

67. A computer repair shop advertises a discount of 15% off all computer repairs. The original cost to repair Robert's computer is $328. How much money will he save, with the discount?

- a. $39.36
- b. $42.64
- c. $45.92
- d. $49.20

68. A professor submits approximately 10 articles every 3 years for publication consideration in various scholarly journals. If this trend continues, which of the following represents the number of articles the professor will submit in a 30-year career?

- a. 30
- b. 90
- c. 100
- d. 300

69. Gitta consumes approximately 56 grams of protein every 4 days. If she continues to consume the same amount of protein, which of the following represents the number of grams of protein she will consume in 30 days?

    a. 360
    b. 420
    c. 380
    d. 400

70. A sequence is formed from the equation, $y = 6x + 2$, where x represents the term number and y represents the value of the term. What is the value of the 18th term in the sequence?

    a. 98
    b. 104
    c. 110
    d. 116

71. Andy has already saved \$15. He plans to save \$28 per month. Which of the following equations represents the amount of money he will have saved in x months?

    a. $y = 15 + 28x$
    b. $y = 43x + 15$
    c. $y = 43x$
    d. $y = 28 + 15x$

72. Which of the following graphs represents the equation, $y = -3x + 8$?

a.
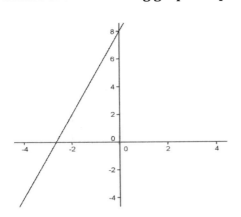

b.
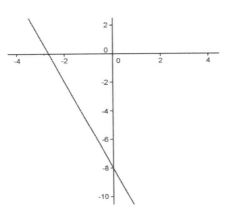

c.
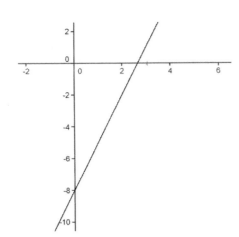

d.
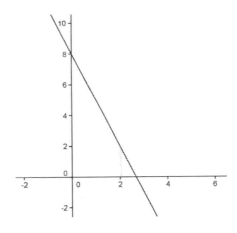

73. The number of parking spaces painted per number of hours is represented in the table below.

Number of Hours	Numbers of Spaces Painted
4	52
7	91
11	143
13	169
16	208

According to the table, how many parking spaces are painted per hour?
  a. 12
  b. 13
  c. 14
  d. 16

74. The cost of Brian's text messaging service per month is $12, plus $0.07 for each text sent. Which of the following tables represents the cost of Brian's monthly bill?

a.

Number of Text Messages Sent	Monthly Cost
0	$12.00
1	$12.07
2	$12.14
3	$12.21
4	$12.28
20	$13.40

c.

Number of Text Messages Sent	Monthly Cost
0	$0
1	$12.00
2	$12.07
3	$12.14
4	$12.21
20	$13.33

b.

Number of Text Messages Sent	Monthly Cost
0	$12.07
1	$12.14
2	$12.21
3	$12.28
4	$12.35
20	$13.47

d.

Number of Text Messages Sent	Monthly Cost
0	$0
1	$12.07
2	$12.14
3	$12.21
4	$12.28
20	$13.33

75. Given a triangle with vertices of A(2, 8), B(4, 8), and C(3, 12), which of the following represents the vertices for a translation of the triangle 6 units up and 3 units to the left?

  a. A'(8, 5), B'(10, 5), C'(9, 9)
  b. A'(8, 11), B'(10, 11), C'(9, 15)
  c. A'(−1, 14), B'(1, 14), C'(0, 18)
  d. A'(−1, 2), B'(1, 2), C'(0, 6)

Science

Science topics are both informative and fascinating. Learning about the amazing diversity of life forms on the planet is one of the most enjoyable parts of school for many students, and for some, biology becomes a life-long pursuit. The same is true about the study of our planet, our solar system, and the universe. Other areas of science are equally as engrossing. There are many difference facets of science, and all of them have an impact on our lives in a myriad of ways. You'll need to do well in this subject in order to earn your high school diploma. Here are some questions that can help you make sure you're on track when it comes to science.

Directions: Use the information below and your knowledge of science to answer questions 1–3.

Consider the following chemical equation, which shows the oxidation of sucrose:

$C_{12}H_{12}O_{11} + 12\ O_2 \rightarrow 12\ CO_2 + 11\ H_2O + energy\ (5.64 \cdot 10^3\ kJ/mol)$

1. Which of the following is a reactant in the equation?

    a. Carbon dioxide
    b. Oxygen
    c. Water
    d. None of these

2. Is the reaction represented by this equation exothermic or endothermic?

    a. Exothermic
    b. Endothermic
    c. Both
    d. Neither

3. According to this equation, if five molecules of sucrose react with 60 molecules of oxygen, how many molecules of water will be produced?

    a. 5
    b. 55
    c. 60
    d. 65

4. What layer of the atmosphere is closest to the Earth?

    a. Ionosphere
    b. Mesosphere
    c. Stratosphere
    d. Troposphere

5. Which of the following correctly describes how atmospheric pressure depends on altitude?

    a. Atmospheric pressure increases with increasing altitude.
    b. Atmospheric pressure decreases with increasing altitude.
    c. Atmospheric pressure first increases up to a certain altitude, then decreases.
    d. Atmospheric pressure does not depend on altitude.

6. Lichen consists of two separate organisms, a fungus and an alga: The alga provides energy through photosynthesis, while the fungus protects the alga and provides minerals. What is this an example of?

    a. Commensalism
    b. Competition
    c. Mutualism
    d. Parasitism

Directions: Use the information below and your knowledge of science to answer questions 7–8.

When two notes are played that have very close (but not identical) frequencies, it sounds like a single note of a constant pitch that gets louder and softer at a beat frequency equal to the difference in the frequencies of the individual sounds.

7. Which of the following wave shapes would correspond to the sound described?

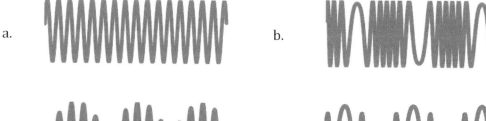

8. Which of the following would decrease the beat frequency of the combined sound?

    a. Lowering the pitch of the higher note
    b. Raising the pitch of the higher note
    c. Lowering the pitch of both notes by the same amount
    d. Raising the pitch of both notes by the same amount

9. The Earth's axis is tilted about 23.5° (relative to a line perpendicular from its plane of rotation). If the Earth's axis were not tilted, which of the following would be true?

    a. There would be no tides.
    b. There would be no day and night.
    c. There would be no seasons.
    d. There would be all of the above.

10. In the nineteenth century, some scientists thought there was a planet even closer to the Sun than Mercury, which they called Vulcan (no relation to the fictional planet Vulcan in *Star Trek*). Further discoveries showed this planet did not exist, but if there were a planet that close to the Sun, which of the following would definitely be true?

    a. It would be denser than Earth.
    b. It would be less dense than Earth.
    c. It would be hotter than Earth.
    d. It would be colder than Earth.

11. What function does the Golgi apparatus serve in a cell?
    a. The Golgi apparatus produces energy.
    b. The Golgi apparatus surrounds the cell and protects it from its environment.
    c. The Golgi apparatus synthesizes proteins out of raw materials.
    d. The Golgi apparatus packages proteins to be sent elsewhere.

12. Looking at a cell through a microscope, a student notices that it contains two separate sets of chromosomes at opposite ends of the cell. What does this indicate about the cell?
    a. The cell is cancerous.
    b. The cell is a white blood cell.
    c. The cell is dying.
    d. The cell is undergoing mitosis.

13. What kind of cell is shown in this diagram?

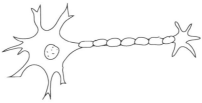

    a. Muscle cell
    b. Nerve cell
    c. Red blood cell
    d. White blood cell

14. What is a substance composed of a single kind of molecule but with more than one chemical element?
    a. A compound
    b. A heterogeneous mixture
    c. A homogeneous mixture
    d. A solution

15. Which of the following is NOT a chemical element?
    a. Copper
    b. Gold
    c. Iron
    d. Steel

16. Igneous rocks are usually formed deep beneath the Earth's crust. Where else can igneous rocks be formed?
    a. Atolls
    b. Mountaintops
    c. Riverbeds
    d. Volcanoes

Directions: Use the information below and your knowledge of science to answer questions 17–20.

A certain type of fast-breeding beetle has either large or small mandibles (jaws). The size of the mandibles is genetic. A student takes a randomly selected sample of beetles from the wild and feeds them exclusively on large, hard-shelled seeds. She records the number of large-mandibled and small-mandibled beetles each month, and gets the following data:

Month:	Number of large-mandibled beetles:	Number of small-mandibled beetles:
1	40	60
2	42	55
3	43	52
4	48	50
5	55	48
6	56	51
7	59	49
8	64	45
9	69	40
10	65	38
11	67	37
12	72	33

17. Which of the following best explains the data?

a. The number of large-mandibled beetles increases because they are best able to cope with the hard-shelled seeds.
b. The number of large-mandibled beetles increases because they are able to fight off and kill the small-mandibled beetles.
c. The number of small-mandibled beetles increases because they are able to reproduce more quickly.
d. The number of small-mandibled beetles increases because there is not enough food to sustain the larger-mandibled beetles.

18. Based on these data, what kind of trait are large mandibles?

a. Dominant
b. Recessive
c. Co-dominant
d. None of these

19. What are the beetles involved in the experiment an example of?

a. A biome
b. A community
c. An ecosystem
d. A population

68

20. Which of the following phyla of animals do beetles belong to?
    a. Annelids
    b. Arthropods
    c. Chordates
    d. Mollusks

21. Some manual generators work by having the user turn a crank; the generator then produces electricity. What kind of energy does the generator convert to electrical energy?
    a. Chemical
    b. Kinetic
    c. Potential
    d. Thermal

22. What is the term for an object that electricity flows through easily?
    a. A capacitor
    b. A conductor
    c. An insulator
    d. A resistor

23. What does this symbol represent in a circuit diagram?

    a. An ammeter
    b. A capacitor
    c. A ground
    d. A resistor

Directions: Use the information below and your knowledge of science to answer questions 24–26.

An environmental scientist measures the iron content of the water at various points in a river. She makes this graph of her data:

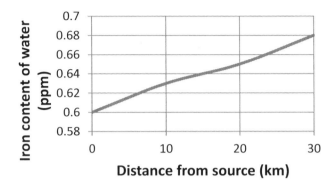

24. Which of the following best explains her data?
    a. The concentration of iron in the river increases because it dissolves more minerals as it flows.
    b. The concentration of iron in the river increases because it gets closer to the source.
    c. The concentration of iron in the river decreases because it deposits minerals as it flows.
    d. The concentration of iron in the river decreases because it gets farther from the source.

25. According to the scientist's data, by about what percentage did the iron content of the water change over the 30 kilometers of her measurements?
    a. 0.08 percent
    b. 8 percent
    c. 13 percent
    d. 400 percent

26. Water flowing in a river is one part of the water cycle. What part of the water cycle could some of the water in the river have gone through immediately before this?
    a. Evaporation
    b. Infiltration
    c. Precipitation
    d. Transpiration

27. What is the collective term for all the water on and in the planet Earth?
    a. The biosphere
    b. The hydrosphere
    c. Panthalassa
    d. The Seven Seas

28. Which of the following is NOT one of the major systems of the human organism?
    a. Digestive system
    b. Muscular system
    c. Regulatory system
    d. Reproductive system

Mometrix

29. The aorta is a large artery that connects to the left ventricle of the heart. Which organ system does the aorta belong to?

    a. Circulatory
    b. Endocrine
    c. Respiratory
    d. Skeletal

Directions: Use the information below and your knowledge of science to answer questions 30–32.

A geologist has a sample containing fermium-253, a radioactive material. He measures the radioactive emissions from the sample once per day over a week and gets the data in this chart.

Day	Radiation
1	2440 MBq
2	1920 MBq
3	1541 MBq
4	1218 MBq
5	970 MBq
6	770 MBq
7	611 MBq

(*MBq* stands for megabecquerels, a unit of radioactivity. The measurement in megabecquerels can be assumed to be proportional to the number of atoms remaining of the radioactive substance.)

30. The half-life of the radioactive material is the time it takes for half the radioactive atoms to decay. From the scientist's data, what is the approximate half-life of fermium-253?

    a. 1 day
    b. 3 days
    c. 1 week
    d. 30 years

31. Which of the following is NOT a type of radiation that can be emitted in radioactive decay?

    a. Alpha radiation
    b. Beta radiation
    c. Gamma rays
    d. X-rays

32. The scientist also measures the mass of the particles. Which of the following tables could show the results of this measurement?

a.

Day	Mass
1	1000 ng
2	990 ng
3	983 ng
4	977 ng
5	972 ng
6	969 ng
7	965 ng

b.

Day	Mass
1	1000 ng
2	794 ng
3	630 ng
4	500 ng
5	397 ng
6	315 ng
7	250 ng

c.

Day	Mass
1	1000 ng
2	1010 ng
3	1017 ng
4	1023 ng
5	1028 ng
6	1031 ng
7	1035 ng

d.

Day	Mass
1	1000 ng
2	1206 ng
3	1370 ng
4	1500 ng
5	1603 ng
6	1685 ng
7	1750 ng

33. In about 6 billion years, what will happen to the Sun?

    a. It will expand into a red giant.
    b. It will collapse into a black hole.
    c. It will explode in a supernova.
    d. It will continue as it is.

34. Which of the following best explains why the moon has so many more craters than the Earth?

    a. The Earth's magnetic field deflects most meteors.
    b. The moon is closer to space, so more meteors hit it.
    c. Craters on the Earth are eventually effaced by erosion and plate tectonics.
    d. The moon is made of a softer substance that forms craters more easily.

Directions: Use the information below and your knowledge of science to answer questions 35–37.

Using a cotton swab, a student takes samples from various surfaces around the school cafeteria and grows them in Petri dishes to see where there are the most germs. He counts the bacterial colonies that grow in each Petri dish and gets this data:

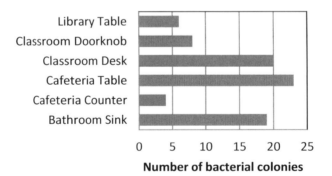

35. Based on these data, which of the following would be most effective in helping decrease diseases at the school?

    a. Cleaning the bathroom sinks regularly
    b. Cleaning the cafeteria tables before meals
    c. Not touching the library tables
    d. Wiping off doorknobs after use

36. Many students at the school come down with the flu at the same time. Could this be explained by the student's data?

    a. Yes, because the student's data show that there are bacteria everywhere in the school

    b. Yes, because the student's data show where the bacteria that cause the flu are most likely to have come from

    c. Not necessarily, because the population of bacteria would change over time

    d. Not necessarily, because the flu is not caused by bacteria

37. What is the term for a sudden large outbreak of disease in a population, as described in question 36?

    a. An antibody

    b. An epidemic

    c. An immunity

    d. An infection

38. If unbalanced forces are acting on an object, which of the following must be true?

    a. The object is speeding up.

    b. The object is slowing down.

    c. The object is changing direction.

    d. Any of the above may be true.

39. Which of the following best describes the difference between mass and weight?

    a. Mass is an inherent property of an object; weight is the force with which gravity pulls it.

    b. An object's weight is equal to its mass divided by its volume.

    c. Weight is an inherent property of an object; mass depends on the force acting on it.

    d. There is no difference; *mass* and *weight* are two words for the same thing.

40. For the first few billion years of the Earth's history, there was almost no molecular oxygen in the atmosphere. Now, the atmosphere is about 21 percent oxygen by volume. What is the primary factor that caused this change?

    a. Early life produced oxygen through photosynthesis.

    b. Oxygen radiated from the Sun built up in the atmosphere.

    c. Oxygen was brought to the Earth on comets and meteors.

    d. Volcanic activity released oxygen from deep inside the Earth.

41. Which of the following best explains why there are few fossils of the earliest life-forms?

    a. Those fossils would have formed so long ago that they would have eroded away by now.

    b. The earliest life-forms lived on the ocean floors, where fossils cannot form easily.

    c. The earliest life-forms did not have bones or other hard parts that would readily fossilize.

    d. Plenty of fossils of the earliest life-forms exist, but they're buried very deeply and hard to reach.

42. When a vervet monkey sees an eagle, it makes a specific alarm call to warn other monkeys nearby. What is this an example of?

    a. A behavioral response

    b. A glandular response

    c. A maladaptation

    d. A parasitic relationship

43. The number of organisms that can survive in an ecosystem depends on both living and nonliving resources and factors. What are the nonliving factors (such as temperature, availability of water, etc.) known as?

    a.   Abiotic factors
    b.   Biotic factors
    c.   Climatic factors
    d.   Dependent factors

Mometrix

Social Studies

Imparting an understanding of humans and the societies and cultures they have created is the goal of social studies classes. This wide ranging field encompasses psychology, religion, economics, politics, anthropology, sociology, law, government, history, geography, and many other topics. No education is complete without a well-rounded course of studies in these areas. You'll find the following questions helpful as you seek to gain deeper insights into the world around you.

Civics/Government

1. What is meant by the term "checks and balances"?

a. The Founding Fathers were committed to having an economically responsible nation and implemented a very rigid budget system.

b. There was concern among the Founding Fathers that the Constitution would not be a perfect legal document; because of this, the document was shown to as many lawyers as possible prior to its publication.

c. The Founding Fathers were wary of the centralized power they knew under King George, so they divided roles of government so that no single branch would hold all of the power.

d. The Founding Fathers knew that debt incurred from the American Revolution would be troublesome; because of this, the Internal Revenue Service (IRS) was created immediately following the war.

2. The Great Compromise refers to which agreement by the Founding Fathers?

a. Having a bicameral legislature wherein states would have equal representation in one house and representation based on state population in the other.

b. That Virginia would be split in two, with West Virginia siding with the Union and Virginia remaining apart of the Confederacy.

c. That a slave would count as three-fifths of a person for purposes of representation and taxation.

d. That the Articles of Confederation was not adequate and that another document was needed.

3. A "veto" refers to the president's constitutional right to do what?

a. Use executive power in lieu of seeking a formal declaration of war

b. Call a special session of Congress to deal with emergencies

c. Reject a bill passed by Congress

d. Suspend certain rights in times of national crisis

4. Which of the following best describes the concept of "implied powers"?

a. Some powers held by the government that are not known by the public

b. Powers not specifically expressed by the Constitution, but that can be inferred from the text

c. That each branch of government is encouraged to suggest how the other should rule

d. That the President's Cabinet has power by association

5. What is the administrative system that serves to govern the United States of America often called?

a. Administration

b. Bureaucracy

c. Plutocracy

d. Cabinet

6. What term did the framers of the Constitution use to explain the sharing of powers by central and state governments?

  a. Republicanism
  b. Democracy
  c. Federalism
  d. Diarchy

7. What is another name for a person seeking to influence an elected official on a particular issue?

  a. Delegate
  b. Lobbyist
  c. Incumbent
  d. Constituent

8. Which of the following best defines judicial review?

  a. The right of federal courts to determine if a law violates the Constitution.
  b. The right of the president to review the sitting justices of the Supreme Court.
  c. An annual publication written by the justices of the Supreme Court.
  d. The right of federal courts to revoke the office of unfit politicians.

9. Who is responsible for appointing Supreme Court judges?

  a. The president
  b. Fellow Supreme Court judges
  c. Both houses of congress
  d. The people of the United States of America by popular vote

10. Which of the following refers to the act of a member of Congress giving long speeches in order to block the passage of certain legislation?

  a. Gerrymander
  b. Pork barrel
  c. Filibuster
  d. Muckraker

11. Which of the following is NOT a function served by a political party?

  a. They manage the nomination of political candidates.
  b. They manage the day-to-day operations of the military.
  c. They serve to mobilize voters.
  d. They serve to bring order to the political process.

12. When powers granted by the Constitution are shared by both state and federal governments, they are known as...

  a. Concurrent powers.
  b. Merged powers.
  c. Combined powers.
  d. Continuous powers.

13. The 10ᵗʰ Amendment grants reserved powers to whom?

    a. The states
    b. The federal government
    c. The president
    d. The Supreme Court

14. Voters should carefully consider the views of the vice president for all of the following reasons EXCEPT...

    a. The vice president provides the deciding vote in the event of a tie vote in the Senate.
    b. In the event that the sitting president is unable to serve, the vice president assumes the role of president.
    c. The vice president frequently meets with other heads of state in a diplomatic role.
    d. The vice president's religious beliefs will affect the religious freedoms of the people.

Geography

1. Which mountain range separates Europe from Asia?

    a. Alps
    b. Pyrenees
    c. Ural Mountains
    d. Blue Ridge Mountains

2. Which of the following countries is NOT in Africa?

    a. Morocco
    b. Togo
    c. Laos
    d. Mozambique

3. Which of the following is an example of an artificial (man-made) waterway?

    a. Canal
    b. Creek
    c. Pond
    d. River

4. The Suez Canal is located in which country?

    a. Ethiopia
    b. Syria
    c. Ukraine
    d. Egypt

5. Which country is NOT a member of the European Union?

    a. Cyprus
    b. Turkey
    c. Slovenia
    d. Estonia

6. Which of the following countries is a subcontinent?

    a. India
    b. Australia
    c. Madagascar
    d. Greenland

7. Which of the following countries is also a continent?

    a. Canada
    b. Russia
    c. Greenland
    d. Australia

8. Which of the following countries was NOT once a Republic of the Soviet Union?

    a. Georgia
    b. Uzbekistan
    c. Poland
    d. Belarus

9. Which of the following countries is part of South America?

    a. Uruguay
    b. Nicaragua
    c. Belize
    d. El Salvador

History

1. The Magna Carta is a historical document that declared what?

    a. The United States was independent from England.
    b. That English citizens were free from punishment except through established law.
    c. That the people of America had the right to religious freedom.
    d. That the people of England had the right to religious freedom,

2. Which of the following was NOT a main reason for the American Revolution?

    a. The Stamp Act that forced colonists to help pay for British troops stationed in America.
    b. The American citizens wanted "no taxation without representation."
    c. The monopoly held by the East India Tea Company that led to the Boston Tea Party.
    d. The French and Indian War.

3. Which of the following iconic institutions was NOT a direct result of the end of slavery in the United States?

    a. 40 Acres and a Mule
    b. The Freedman's Bureau
    c. Uncle Tom's Cabin by Harriet Beecher Stowe
    d. The 13th Amendment

4. Which of the following states was still a territory during the Civil War?

    a. Nebraska
    b. Tennessee
    c. Wisconsin
    d. Texas

5. The assassination of Archduke Franz Ferdinand of Austria-Hungary triggered which war?

    a. The Seven Years' War
    b. World War I
    c. World War II
    d. The Austro-Prussian War

6. The Allied Forces of World War II were comprised of which countries?

    a. The United States, Poland, the Soviet Union, and Italy
    b. Germany, France, Japan and Italy
    c. The United States, Great Britain, the Soviet Union, and Australia
    d. Germany, Poland, Switzerland and France

7. Which of the following ideologies led directly to World War II?

    a. Nationalism
    b. Communism
    c. Socialism
    d. Fascism

8. Which of the following was the leader of the National Fascist Party during World War II?

    a. Joseph Stalin
    b. Adolf Hitler
    c. Leon Trotsky
    d. Benito Mussolini

9. What was a powerful result of the California Gold Rush?

    a. California's population exploded and new cities were formed.
    b. Hundreds of thousands of Native Americans were killed or displaced.
    c. Travel sped up with the development of transcontinental railroads and steamships.
    d. All of the above

10. In what ways were children in Western Territories afforded opportunities for education?

    a. They were homeschooled by their parents.
    b. They attended one-room schoolhouses when weather and farming schedules permitted.
    c. They sent away for educational materials and learned by correspondence.
    d. All of the above

Economics

1. What is the most likely outcome of the cost of coffee beans from South America rising?

    a. The United States boycotts South American coffee.
    b. Starbucks raises their prices to accommodate the new cost.
    c. There is a proportionate rise in the amount of traffic accidents caused by drowsiness.
    d. American households switch to tea for their morning drink.

2. Antitrust laws are most accurately associated with which of the following?

    a. Monopolies
    b. Corruption
    c. Deflation
    d. Railroads

3. What federal agency is responsible for protecting consumers while maintaining free and fair competition in the marketplace?
   a. Internal Revenue Service
   b. Federal Bureau of Investigation
   c. Environmental Protection Agency
   d. Federal Trade Commission

4. What is another name for a certificate issued by the government that promises to repay borrowed money at a fixed interest rate?
   a. Concession
   b. Tax
   c. Bond
   d. Tribute

5. Entrepreneurism refers to what?
   a. The first business in a new market
   b. The organization, management, and risk of a business taken on by an individual
   c. The first business in a new industry
   d. Research and development conducted by existing businesses

6. The federal budget consists of revenues and expenditures. What is an example of revenue?
   a. Fines and penalties
   b. Taxes
   c. Loans
   d. All of the above

7. Which of the following is a service provided by almost all banks and credit unions?
   a. Setting interest rates
   b. Making loans at interest
   c. Printing currency
   d. All of the above

8. What is the primary purpose behind the government's prevention of monopolies?
   a. To disrupt unhealthy growth
   b. To encourage a competitive market
   c. To keep any one company from achieving influence that might rival the federal government
   d. To keep the market in line with the government's monetary policy

9. What organization carries out the United States of America's monetary policy?
   a. The Central Bank
   b. The Internal Revenue Service
   c. The House Committee on Ways and Means
   d. The Federal Reserve

10. The downturn of economies across the world following the 2008 recession in the United States is an example of what?

    a. The weakness of other economies
    b. The need for a universal currency
    c. The interdependence of the world market
    d. The lack of predictability in the world market

Vocabulary Practice

Words are the very foundation, the building blocks, of human communication. Whether we're speaking or writing, we're expressing a message to another human being by choosing certain words to convey our intended meaning. All the words that a person knows make up their vocabulary. The more words you know, the better you'll be when it comes to making your meaning clear to others. People will understand you more clearly when you can choose from several words with different shades of meaning to make your thoughts clear. You'll be better at describing things, which will be very useful in many different ways. Of course, this works both ways – when you have an extensive vocabulary, you'll be much better equipped to understand written and spoken communications from others. When you understand the meaning of lots of words, you'll do better on tests, in job interviews, and in many other important areas of life. And don't ever forget that improving your vocabulary is something you never stop doing. It's a life-long process. The following exercise will help you improve your vocabulary.

For each sentence, choose the answer that is the closest in meaning to the word in italics.

1. **The cabin is quite *secluded*.**

    a. cozy
    b. large
    c. beautiful
    d. private

2. **Our son hopes to go to school to study *aeronautics*.**

    a. advanced level math
    b. birds and their environments
    c. repairing and installing air conditioners
    d. building airplanes and rockets

3. **The house has a *stucco* exterior with a shingle roof.**

    a. dark brown
    b. fine plaster
    c. brick
    d. aluminum siding

4. **He behaved in a *petulant* manner.**

    a. like a trained professional
    b. like a dog or cat
    c. like an angry child
    d. like a mature adult

5. **My mother says she might *boycott* the new store.**

    a. refuse to shop there
    b. shop there a lot
    c. design the interior
    d. get a job at

Mometrix

6. We learned about that *epoch* in class yesterday.

    a. large mountain range
    b. important period of time
    c. very strong glue
    d. portion of the bottom of the ocean

7. His story was *plausible*.

    a. obviously false
    b. very sad
    c. believable
    d. beautiful

8. My uncle seems to think he's an *aristocrat*.

    a. a person who's an expert on something
    b. a person who lives in another country
    c. a person who's very skilled at something
    d. a person who's superior to others

9. Her performance at the recital was *phenomenal*.

    a. extraordinary
    b. average
    c. terrible
    d. the last one

10. I don't really like *contemporary* music.

    a. played on a piano
    b. old
    c. modern
    d. extremely loud

11. I wish you wouldn't *avert* your eyes when we talk.

    a. turn away
    b. blink rapidly
    c. close
    d. rub vigorously

12. My grandfather is *eccentric*.

    a. overweight
    b. old
    c. talkative
    d. unusual

13. Her *hostile* attitude was obvious to everyone.

    a. friendly
    b. unfriendly
    c. mellow
    d. neutral

14. That material is too *porous* for our project.

    a. expensive
    b. full of tiny holes
    c. irregularly shaped
    d. very fragile

15. Your *endeavors* made a real difference.

    a. monetary gifts
    b. prayers
    c. efforts
    d. friends and family

16. Read the book *excerpt* before taking the quiz.

    a. review of
    b. table of contents
    c. description of
    d. short passage from

17. His *effigy* was displayed in the public square for a week.

    a. a sculpture or doll resembling a person
    b. a person's name written in fancy handwriting
    c. a championship trophy
    d. exhibit of paintings

18. At times, my Aunt Jenny can be *irascible*.

    a. extremely funny
    b. easily irritated
    c. very sad
    d. extremely talkative

19. We should get together and *reminisce*.

    a. make plans for a project
    b. cook a gourmet meal
    c. talk about the past
    d. go hiking in the wilderness

20. We will need to *emphasize* that at the meeting.

    a. vote on
    b. make very important
    c. ignore
    d. discuss at length

21. The discussion grew increasingly *strident*.

    a. loud and harsh
    b. soft and quiet
    c. boring
    d. focused on unimportant matters

Mometrix

22. **The jigsaw puzzle turned out to be very *intricate*.**

    a. large
    b. beautiful to look at
    c. easy to figure out
    d. complicated

23. **His *valor* will be talked remembered for centuries.**

    a. butler
    b. driver
    c. bravery
    d. lack of intelligence

24. **The *elegy* really captured Tom's spirit.**

    a. sad poem at a funeral
    b. an oil painting of a person
    c. humorous short story
    d. a play about a person's life

25. **Some people tend to *denigrate* people they disagree with.**

    a. physically attack
    b. convert to a different opinion
    c. ignore
    d. say bad things about

26. **You have *myriad* choices when it comes to restaurants.**

    a. very few
    b. a great number
    c. more than 5, but less than 10
    d. two dozen

27. **Our decision to go to a movie was *spontaneous*.**

    a. not very smart
    b. agreed to by everyone
    c. spur of the moment
    d. made in advance

28. **Make sure you use *indelible* ink.**

    a. impossible to remove
    b. can't be seen in ordinary light
    c. inexpensive
    d. very dark blue

29. **Here's a *memento* for you.**

    a. a piece of gourmet cheese
    b. an object to remind one of something
    c. the filling inside of an olive
    d. a Canadian silver dollar

85

Copyright © Mometrix Media. You have been licensed one copy of this document for personal use only. Any other reproduction or redistribution is strictly prohibited. All rights reserved.
This content is provided for test preparation purposes only and does not imply an endorsement by Mometrix of any particular political, scientific, or religious point of view.

30. That is outside my *sphere* of expertise.

   a. area
   b. book
   c. triangle
   d. knowledge

31. To me, something's not art if it isn't *tangible*.

   a. can be easily sold
   b. one of a kind
   c. can be touched
   d. very old

32. You can know something's *velocity*, or its exact location, but not both.

   a. atomic structure
   b. speed
   c. direction
   d. place of origin

33. The R&D department is our company's main *sinew*.

   a. source of strength
   b. weak area
   c. very expensive component
   d. claim to fame

34. The meeting was very *boisterous*.

   a. made up mostly of males
   b. long and boring
   c. loud and unruly
   d. effective at solving a problem

35. Mrs. Benson gives quizzes on a *sporadic* basis.

   a. daily
   b. weekly
   c. biweekly
   d. irregular

36. They mayor said the councilman's proposal is too *audacious*.

   a. complicated
   b. bold
   c. ineffective
   d. late

37. Did Benjamin Franklin ever use a *pseudonym*?

   a. large umbrella
   b. false name
   c. fancy carriage
   d. eye doctor

38. I will *enumerate* my reasons for this action later.

   a. list
   b. think about
   c. cover up
   d. deny

39. Your design may be a bit too *ornate*.

   a. plain
   b. unoriginal
   c. fancy
   d. expensive

40. I will *swelter* if I sit by the window.

   a. be very cold
   b. be very hot
   c. be comfortable
   d. become sleepy

41. Mr. Benevides made his *disdain* clear.

   a. happiness
   b. confusion
   c. anger
   d. contempt

42. Mike, it will be your task to *convey* all the materials.

   a. replace
   b. transport
   c. purchase
   d. re-arrange

Spelling

Spelling is very important, because words are the foundation of written communication. If words aren't spelled correctly, several things can happen, and none of them are good. Poor spelling always hampers the processing of the written information on the part of the reader. When readers run across a misspelled word, they mentally pause as their brain notes the misspelling. If the word is so badly spelled that they don't know what word was intended, they have to stop and wonder what the writer actually meant. Worse, sometimes the word is misspelled in a way that readers take it for a completely different word, which can lead to terrible misunderstandings. Finally, poor spelling gives readers the impression that the writer is poorly educated. This can make it difficult to succeed in a career, and in many other aspects of life. It's important to master the art of good spelling. This exercise will help you become a better speller.

Spelling Exercise

Each question contains four words for you to consider. If one of them is misspelled, circle it. If they are all spelled correctly, circle NO MISTAKES.

1.	potential	arroneous	familiar	pajamas	NO MISTAKES
2.	hazzard	limousine	obsolete	franchise	NO MISTAKES
3.	morgage	compelled	radius	thoroughly	NO MISTAKES
4.	stimulus	resede	calligraphy	precipice	NO MISTAKES
5.	subordinate	amass	sentimeter	junction	NO MISTAKES
6.	religious	fertilize	subscribe	mischievious	NO MISTAKES
7.	venom	mersonary	longevity	diagnosis	NO MISTAKES
8.	silhouette	comemorate	hesitant	lunatic	NO MISTAKES
9.	circulate	connasewer	judicial	paralyze	NO MISTAKES
10.	sermise	susceptible	moccasin	unnecessary	NO MISTAKES
11.	lunar	sophomore	coladeral	trespassing	NO MISTAKES
12.	narrater	antique	liaison	extravagant	NO MISTAKES
13.	asterisk	aerial	vertigo	meticulus	NO MISTAKES
14.	carburetor	acidic	qwixotic	amorous	NO MISTAKES
15.	acquit	intramural	jurer	antidote	NO MISTAKES
16.	allotted	meteor	regime	grotesk	NO MISTAKES
17.	miracle	asthma	envious	dillemma	NO MISTAKES
18.	neutral	infernal	sieve	undooly	NO MISTAKES
19.	malody	chameleon	symbol	cymbal	NO MISTAKES
20.	condemn	snorkel	abstane	politically	NO MISTAKES
21.	fiery	ashphalt	bachelor	delicate	NO MISTAKES
22.	deceive	anikdote	schedule	catastrophe	NO MISTAKES
23.	vetaran	veterinarian	obesity	remotely	NO MISTAKES
24.	access	eccessive	tranquil	verbose	NO MISTAKES
25.	circular	insufficient	oncore	safari	NO MISTAKES
26.	cancel	acumulate	geography	hindrance	NO MISTAKES
27.	neglect	paucity	deffective	magnificent	NO MISTAKES
28.	absorbent	flammable	haphazard	eddible	NO MISTAKES
29.	comerse	flexible	deterrent	biological	NO MISTAKES
30.	cinamun	poignant	relieved	outrageous	NO MISTAKES
31.	elegance	dialogue	arkeology	colonel	NO MISTAKES
32.	deranged	rancid	corperal	moisture	NO MISTAKES
33.	legitimate	unique	nuisance	jenuine	NO MISTAKES

| 34. | adjusted | undoubtedly | devinity | equilibrium | NO MISTAKES |
| 35. | axis | community | whispered | borometer | NO MISTAKES |

Capitalization

Capital letters are very important in written English. They can be used to show respect to people, to identify certain things, and to show that a new sentence has begun. Some words, such as *February* or *Jupiter*, need to be capitalized every time you use them. Other words, like *judge* or *doctor*, are only capitalized in certain situations. For this reason, there are rules to help you remember which words need capitalization. Capitalization can be confusing, so a good rule of thumb is that words are capitalized if they are unique persons, places or things (nouns), if they start a sentence, or if they are part of a person's or thing's title.

Some quick capitalization rules – all these should be capitalized:

- The first word of every sentence
- The first word of a quote
- Names of persons, months, days, holidays, countries, states, and cities
- Initials used in names and well-known organizations
- The word "I"
- Titles of books, songs, or people

This exercise will help you improve your capitalization skills. For each numbered item, read each sentence, and then decide if all of them are capitalized correctly, or if one is capitalized incorrectly. If one of the sentences is capitalized incorrectly, select the letter of the sentence which contains the mistake. If all of them are capitalized correctly, choose NO MISTAKES. Sentences may contain words that aren't capitalized that should be, words that are capitalized that shouldn't be, or both.

1.

    a. Ben Franklin said, "early to bed, early to rise, makes a man healthy, wealthy and wise."
    b. March and April are my favorite months of the year.
    c. I'm very pleased to meet you, Reverend Perez.
    d. NO MISTAKES

2.

    a. No matter what you do, Father Time eventually catches up with you.
    b. Didn't your Father attend college in Europe , Wendell?
    c. We watched Father of the Bride on DVD last night.
    d. NO MISTAKES

3.

    a. Tarrant County Community College's main campus is located in Fort Worth, Texas.
    b. College graduates usually have higher paying jobs than people without degrees.
    c. My older brother is thinking about enrolling in a Community College.
    d. NO MISTAKES

4.

    a. My Uncle Frank has a Doberman Pinscher who is very friendly.
    b. Popular Breeds of dogs include German Shepherds, Labrador Retrievers, and Boxers.
    c. I think Golden Retrievers are beautiful.
    d. NO MISTAKES

5.

    a.   The Republican Party can trace its beginnings back to Abe Lincoln.

    b.   The halloween party for the class will be this Friday, kids.

    c.   Class, remember, GOP stands for Grand Old Party.

    d.   NO MISTAKES

6.

    a.   Sally said her Mom will pick her up after practice is over.

    b.   As Coach Jones always says, "Practice makes perfect, but only if you give it your all."

    c.   Coach Jones and Principal Bronson are in a meeting right now.

    d.   NO MISTAKES

7.

    a.   New York City is full of tourist attractions.

    b.   You could never take in all the interesting sights in New York City in your entire life.

    c.   The statue of liberty is one of the top attractions in the City.

    d.   NO MISTAKES

8.

    a.   The Colorado Rockies are my favorite baseball team.

    b.   My parents took us to Colorado for vacation last year.

    c.   Hey, Steve, this Summer let's visit the Rocky Mountains.

    d.   NO MISTAKES

9.

    a.   Pro athletes, such as football players, are paid a lot of money.

    b.   Our local team's quarterback makes $10 million a year.

    c.   If you ask me, nfl players make way too much money.

    d.   NO MISTAKES

10.

    a.   I don't like Algebra, but I like history and social studies.

    b.   Our French teacher said the final exam will count for half our grade.

    c.   I'm not really a visual person, so geometry is hard for me.

    d.   NO MISTAKES

11.

    a.   Boy, that history test was hard!

    b.   I heard that algebra 2 is very hard to get an A in.

    c.   Cindy, you can do better than a C in Spanish.

    d.   NO MISTAKES

12.

    a.   Fort Worth's motto is "Where the West Begins."

    b.   They call New York City the big apple for a very good reason!

    c.   We saw a plaque marking the Continental Divide.

    d.   NO MISTAKES

13.

    a. Don't miss the Capitol Building when you visit Washington, DC.
    b. We saw the play "Now, That's a Capital Idea!" last night.
    c. The Capital of the European country of France is Paris.
    d. NO MISTAKES

14.

    a. Mercury, Mars, and Venus are the smallest of all the Planets.
    b. I can't believe there's a Planet Hollywood in Myrtle Beach!
    c. It's Yertle the Turtle, not Myrtle the Turtle.
    d. NO MISTAKES

15.

    a. I caught my first fish last year on our family camping trip.
    b. I saw my first hawk when we stopped at our uncle's ranch.
    c. I saw my first broadway play last year on our class trip.
    d. NO MISTAKES

16.

    a. The whole family sang "happy birthday" at the top of our lungs!
    b. I hope you have a happy birthday!
    c. Happy birthday, Dad!
    d. NO MISTAKES

17.

    a. President Obama will arrive soon on his plane, air force one.
    b. The new president of the college will hold a press conference at noon.
    c. The College of William and Mary is located in Williamsburg, Virginia.
    d. NO MISTAKES

18.

    a. The Congresswoman's remarks were printed in the Federal Register.
    b. Did Thomas Jefferson write the Federalist Papers?
    c. I wrote to my Congressman about out of control Federal Spending.
    d. NO MISTAKES

19.

    a. The skyscraper at Sixty-Seven Main Street will be demolished.
    b. Our address is 1419 East Maple Avenue.
    c. The main street in town has four lanes.
    d. NO MISTAKES

20.

    a. Uncle Bob and Aunt Ramona have been married for 40 years.
    b. Uncle Bob said I'm his favorite nephew.
    c. Aunt Ramona said her Uncle is 100 years old.
    d. NO MISTAKES

21.

    a. We went to visit the Henry Ford Museum last Saturday.

    b. We saw an antique Ford model t on display there.

    c. The museum is located in Dearborn, Michigan.

    d. NO MISTAKES

22.

    a. One of my favorite breakfast meals is eggs benedict.

    b. For Mom's birthday, I made scrambled eggs for breakfast in bed.

    c. My parents want to open a bed and breakfast when they get older.

    d. NO MISTAKE

23.

    a. Jimmy doesn't like Cream of Wheat.

    b. Who would ever dream of ordering cereal at International House of Pancakes?

    c. Jimmy I both like Pancakes, and we both like Sausage.

    d. NO MISTAKES

24.

    a. Cook county is where Chicago, Illinois, is located.

    b. Chicago is not just a big city; it's the county seat, too.

    c. The Chicago Bulls have won several NBA championships.

    d. NO MISTAKES

25.

    a. Together we'll form an army of voters and take back the White House!

    b. The Army, Air Force, Navy, and Marines are all military Organizations.

    c. Alex's older brother just enlisted in the Air Force.

    d. NO MISTAKES

26.

    a. "The Wind in the willows" is one of the best books I have ever read.

    b. Most of the books I've read have come from Willowbrook Public Library.

    c. Do you live near a public library?

    d. NO MISTAKES

27.

    a. My dad loves to watch cooking shows on the Food Network.

    b. My dad took Mom and me to a fancy French restaurant.

    c. My dad once ate an entire Pepperoni Pizza by himself!

    d. NO MISTAKES

28.

    a. Dear Mom and Dad, congratulations on your upcoming Anniversary!

    b. This Friday, October 21st, will be my parents' 25th anniversary.

    c. My parents got married 25 years ago at Second Baptist Church.

    d. NO MISTAKES

29.
- a. Who first referred to New Orleans as the Big Easy?
- b. New Orleans is famous for its Jazz Music.
- c. New Orleans was hit hard by Hurricane Katrina.
- d. NO MISTAKES

Punctuation

Good spelling skills and good grammar skills are essential in proper written communications. However, there are other factors that are part of expressing yourself using the written word, and punctuation is one of them. Good punctuation is a vital component of written communication. It helps the reader to interpret the message correctly, without getting confused or having to re-read it several times to decipher the message.

For each question, choose the text that is not punctuated correctly. If all are punctuated correctly, choose NO MISTAKES.

1.

    a. We'll be visiting Boston, and New York City.
    b. Stop, thief!
    c. Mr. and Mrs. Smith said they love their new home.
    d. NO MISTAKES

2.

    a. "Billy," said his mother, "take out the trash."
    b. The dog, eager for a walk brought his leash to his master.
    c. It's finally beginning to feel like summer.
    d. NO MISTAKES

3.

    a. Once upon a time there lived a lonely princess.
    b. We need eggs; milk; and bread.
    c. That's easy for you to say, Pedro.
    d. NO MISTAKES

4.

    a. The principal shook my hand and congratulated me.
    b. Once bitten, twice shy.
    c. Theres no time like the present for making changes.
    d. NO MISTAKES

5.

    a. The kitten loves to chase it's tail.
    b. It began raining, so we called off the ball game.
    c. You'll need the following items: hat, gloves, and parka.
    d. NO MISTAKES

6.

    a. When it rains, it pours.
    b. Mrs. Smiths' cat had six kittens last night.
    c. Did your brothers win their football game?
    d. NO MISTAKES

7.

    a. Now, if you'll excuse me, I must be going.
    b. This is my little brother – Tommy.
    c. "It's a long way to Tipperary."
    d. NO MISTAKES

8.

    a. He asked, "Mom, do you need any help with the groceries"?
    b. That's right; I got a perfect score on my algebra test.
    c. Sit down this instant, young man!
    d. NO MISTAKES

9.

    a. Robert; would you please mail this letter for me?
    b. In this situation, patience is the best strategy.
    c. Dad said, "We should leave soon to beat the traffic."
    d. NO MISTAKES

10.

    a. There are all kinds of people in the world.
    b. Hermione, that's a terrific idea:
    c. What's the good word?
    d. NO MISTAKES

11.

    a. Please make sure each dog has its own food bowl.
    b. He hit the ball and ran very-quickly toward first base.
    c. It's only May and it's already 90 degrees?
    d. NO MISTAKES

12.

    a. I believe Americas best days are still to come.
    b. There's a pie in the oven for dessert.
    c. I'd like to request a seat by the window, please.
    d. NO MISTAKES

13.

    a. Edgar Allan Poe was one of the greatest poet's who ever lived.
    b. It will be faster if we take the elevator.
    c. Don't worry; everything will work out just fine.
    d. NO MISTAKES

14.

    a. This is my pet hamster, Desdemona.
    b. I believe "Inez, we'll meet on the steps at 3" were her exact words.
    c. 3 time's 15 equals 45.
    d. NO MISTAKES

15.

    a. "Well, Cindy," Mrs. Gomez replied, "that's a very good question."
    b. You really – and I know it's difficult – need to calm down a little bit.
    c. The umpire cried, "You're out!"
    d. NO MISTAKES

16.

    a. What does "one if by land, and two if by sea", mean?
    b. Senator Jones, who grew up here, will be visiting next Tuesday.
    c. Here comes a tornado!
    d. NO MISTAKES

17.

    a. George Washington said, "I cannot tell a lie."
    b. If you'd like, we can go to the library Saturday.
    c. My mother (and father) have been married for 15 years.
    d. NO MISTAKES

18.

    a. The old proverb "Look before you leap" is still excellent advice.
    b. The Jones's front lawn earned them a city beautification award last year.
    c. Except for absolute emergencies, you should never be late.
    d. NO MISTAKES

19.

    a. Two cats, one dog, and three hamsters share our house.
    b. Dr. Jones, we'd love to have you over for dinner one evening.
    c. That new song is the cats meow.
    d. NO MISTAKES

20.

    a. If you break it; you must replace it.
    b. What's all the excitement about, anyway?
    c. Did you hear about the snowstorm that's headed our way?
    d. NO MISTAKE

21.

    a. The paper said the plaintiff was very satisfied with the settlement.
    b. The paper described Mrs. Irving as being very satisfied with the settlement.
    c. The paper "described the plaintiff" as being very satisfied with the settlement.
    d. NO MISTAKES

22.

    a. The hippopotamus, and the elephant, are two of the biggest land animals.
    b. Taking up someone's time by being late is very rude.
    c. If you miss school because of illness, you'll need to bring a note from a parent.
    d. NO MISTAKES

23.

    a. Who said "waste not, want not"?

    b. After 20 losses in a row, its about time to hire a new coach.

    c. Why, that's the most ridiculous thing I've ever heard.

    d. NO MISTAKES

24.

    a. Shiver me timbers!

    b. Quiet on the set!

    c. All, aboard!

    d. NO MISTAKES

25.

    a. "Alright," said the coach, "let's get started."

    b. Frank loves his mom's cooking, his favorite dessert is her apple pie.

    c. Worn out from hiking all day, the kids quickly fell asleep.

    d. NO MISTAKES

26.

    a. Everyone likes the new student even though he rarely talks.

    b. I like pizza, more than hamburgers.

    c. We've got a butcher, a baker, and a candlestick maker.

    d. NO MISTAKES

27.

    a. Take two aspirin: and call me in the morning.

    b. No, I don't believe I'll be able to attend.

    c. That's correct; I wear size 10 shoes.

    d. NO MISTAKES

28.

    a. Class, there will be a quiz on the material this Friday.

    b. I can't believe I got a ticket on my bicycle for ignoring a "stop sign."

    c. Harriet, please set the table for dinner.

    d. NO MISTAKES

29.

    a. Mr. Silverman's son is in his final year of law school in New York City.

    b. After giving a bunch of reasons for not going, Dad suddenly changed his mind.

    c. I had no idea that wedding-cakes are so expensive.

    d. NO MISTAKES.

Practice Test Answers and Explanations

Reading

1. C: The correct answer choice is C because paragraphs 2-5 introduce Buck and the setting in which he lives. The paragraphs accomplish this introduction by giving many detailed facts, such as the detail in paragraph 5 about the times he escorted Mollie and Alice on walks. Choice A is incorrect because two new characters, Manuel and the stranger, are introduced in paragraphs 7 and 8. While aspects of paragraphs 2-5 show Buck's personality, choice B is incorrect because the paragraphs also give other details about Buck, such as information about his parents and appearance. Choice D is incorrect because Toots and Ysabel are only mentioned in paragraphs 3 and 4. Furthermore, paragraph 4 says that he utterly ignored Toots and Ysabel, not that he is affectionate towards them.

2. B: The correct answer is choice B because the sentence indicates that Buck felt as if he owned or ruled over Judge Miller's place. The word *realm* indicates that the sentence is referring to everything. Choice A is incorrect because it talks about other dogs that came and went but does not show Buck's attitude towards them or Judge Miller's place. Choice C is incorrect because it shows Buck's opinion of himself but not his opinion of Judge Miller's place. Choice A is incorrect because it describes something that Buck enjoys, but does not give his attitude about the house and grounds at Judge Miller's.

3. B: The correct answer is choice B because details in the passage foreshadow what might happen to Buck. Phrases like "trouble was brewing" or "these men wanted dogs" indicate that one of the dogs men want or Buck might be heading for trouble. Choice A is incorrect because the paragraph does not give details about Buck's life; later paragraphs give those details. Choice C is incorrect because the paragraph does not give setting details. Setting details about Buck's current situation are given in later paragraphs. Choice D is incorrect because the paragraph does not describe any characters other than Buck; it does not indicate that Buck is the villain.

4. A: Choice A is the correct answer because the Klondike strike has caused people to look for dogs like Buck. Although paragraph 1 does not directly mention the Klondike strike, the reader can infer from paragraph 6 that the events discussed refer to the Klondike strike. Choice B is incorrect because paragraph 3 makes it clear that dogs came and went even before the Klondike strike. Choice C is incorrect because Elmo is Buck's father but not a main character in the story. Choice D is incorrect because the passage does not draw a connection between the Klondike strike and the frequency of the Raisin Growers' Association's meetings.

5. D: Choice D is correct because the sentence indicates that Buck considers himself to be like a king. Kings or royalty are often considered regal. Choice A is incorrect because nothing in the paragraph indicates that Buck is scared; in fact, Buck is like a king, which makes him unlikely to be scared of the other dogs. Choice B is incorrect because Buck doesn't indicate anger, which could be shown by barking or growling. Choice C is incorrect because *regal* is referring to Buck feeling like a king, which is unrelated to his happiness.

6. C: Choice C is correct because the first part of the passage mostly describes Buck's life, but the passage ends in a moment of change when the stranger wraps a piece of rope around Buck's neck. Choice A is incorrect because the passage does not describe a sequence of events as they happen. Instead the passage gives an overview of how Buck lived before the moment of change. Although part of the passage describes Buck's history, the passage also describes the moment in which his life

99

changes, making choice B incorrect. Choice D is incorrect because the passage only describes life at Judge Miller's place but doesn't describe what came afterwards.

7. A: The correct answer is choice A because most of the passage provides background information about Buck's life and personality. Choice B is incorrect because the passage does not describe any moments in which Buck is acting heroic; instead, it describes Buck's regular interactions with the other people and animals at Judge Miller's place. Choice C is incorrect because the passage only briefly mentions the Klondike strike. The majority of the passage describes Buck's life. Choice D is incorrect because the other dogs are described in paragraphs 3 and 4. The rest of the passage focuses on Buck.

8. C: The correct answer is choice C because the stranger ties a rope around Buck's neck. This action indicates that Buck will be forced to leave Judge Miller's place. Choice A is incorrect because the end of the passage indicates that Buck might be forced to leave Judge Miller's place, which means he won't be able to continue to act like a king. Choice B is incorrect because the passage does not mention Buck or Shep at the end; Buck's parents are only mentioned in paragraph 5 when the passage describes Buck's family background. Although Manuel is a gardener, choice D is incorrect because Buck is likely leaving the garden to go away with the stranger, which means he won't be able to spend more time in the garden.

9. A: The best answer is choice A because the passage begins by setting up Buck's life and then showing a moment where his life is about to drastically change. Choice B is incorrect because only paragraph 5 refers to family; this is not a big enough portion of the passage to imply that the larger selection is about family. Although Buck might need to work hard in the future, choice C is incorrect because the passage does not have that many clues about upcoming hard work. Choice C is incorrect because the passage does not spend time showing that Buck strongly values relationships. The end of the passage indicates that Buck is about to experience a moment of change.

10. B: The best answer is choice B because paragraph 2 describes Judge Miller's place in great detail, including a description of the house, the driveway, the stables, and the outhouses. Choice A is incorrect because the paragraph only says that his place is in the Santa Clara Valley; however, the paragraph does not describe the valley in detail (it only describes it as sun-kissed). Choice C is incorrect because paragraphs 3 and 4 describe Buck's lifestyle, not paragraph 2. Choice D is incorrect because paragraph 2 does not mention the Klondike strike. The strike is referred to in paragraphs 1 and 6.

11. B: The correct answer is choice B because the sentence talks about how the men want dogs; the sentence foreshadows that Buck may be the type of dog that the men want. Choice A is incorrect because it refers to Buck's attitude around Judge Miller's place but does not hint at what might be coming next. Although part of the sentence indicates that Buck hopes to follow in Elmo's footsteps, the rest of the sentence simply describes Buck's father. Choice B better foreshadows what's going to happen in the story because it more closely relates to the events in paragraph 7 and 8. Choice D is incorrect because the sentence describes Buck's personality and interests without giving clues about what's going to happen next.

12. D: The best answer is choice D because, as a dog, Buck can't read. Although Buck may not be interested in current events, choice A is incorrect because choice D is a more logical answer. Choices B and C are also incorrect because the logic that Buck doesn't read the newspapers is drawn from the fact that dogs can't read.

13. C: The correct answer is C because Andy and his family were in good spirits, or happy, when he left for school at the beginning of the term. Now that he's returned, he knows something is wrong, but isn't sure what it is. Choice A is incorrect because the passage does not discuss Andy's eye color. The phrase *different eyes* is used metaphorically and does not literally mean that Andy has different eyes. For this reason, choice B is also incorrect. Choice D is incorrect because Andy is uneasy rather than happy. He knows something bad has happened.

14. A: Choice A is the correct answer because the phrase *a heavy blow* refers to the very difficult situation that Andy's father now finds himself in. The difficult situation hit him like a hammer, or heavy blow, because it was sudden and very financially painful. While it's true that Andy can't go back to school, choice B is incorrect because the sentence refers to Andy's father rather than Andy. Although losing six thousand dollars is part of the heavy blow, choice C is incorrect because the sentence does not show how much money Andy's father lost. The reader finds out the amount of money in paragraph 11, while the sentence in the question does not appear until paragraph 14. Choice D is incorrect because the sentence does not refer to Andy.

15. D: While parts of the other answer choices are correct, the best answer is choice D because it is the only choice that correctly summarizes the passage. Choice A is incorrect because Andy's father has not won six thousand dollars; he has lost that amount of money. Choice B is incorrect because Nathan Lawrence has stolen twenty thousand dollars, but only six thousand of that amount belonged to Andy's father. Choice C is incorrect because Andy is not cheerful that he doesn't have to go back to school; he likes school and is very disappointed.

16. B: The reader learns in paragraph 1 that Andy likes school. When Andy finds out he can't return to school, he is disappointed but he makes his voice sound cheerful when he's speaking to his family. Choice A is incorrect because it doesn't show Andy's feelings; it just shows that Andy knows how the family's misfortune will affect his studies. Choice C is incorrect because it simply contains Andy's new plans for the future and does not show his emotions. Choice D is incorrect even though this sentence does show Andy's emotions. However, this sentence refers to Andy's opinion about Squire Carter and not about returning to school.

17. D: Choice D is the correct answer. In paragraph 19, Frank says that he didn't agree to pay for both dinners, and then in paragraph 23 he asks for at least ten cents back. These two examples show that Frank thought Mr. Percy would return some of his money. Choice A is incorrect because Frank didn't intend to give all his money even though it may have been generous for Frank to buy Mr. Percy a drink. Choice B is incorrect because Mr. Percy didn't offer to pay for anything; in fact, he took money and didn't repay it. Choice C is incorrect because the passage does not indicate that Mr. Percy owes the money. Instead, it shows Mr. Percy tricking Frank in order to get Frank to buy him drinks.

18. B: The correct answer is choice B because the word *capital* refers to money. The reader can use the context of the passage to find the meaning of *capital*. Frank lost his twenty-five cents, which means his capital had vanished. Even though *capital* refers to money, choice A is incorrect because Frank had twenty-five cents rather than just a penny. Choice C is incorrect because Mr. Percy is the one who calls Frank virtuous. Choice D is incorrect because it's not clear if Frank had a friendship with Mr. Percy in the first place. Therefore, his friendship would not have vanished.

19. C: Frank knew he did not have much money, but when he saw that he would get a free lunch if he bought a drink, he was willing to eat it. Even though Mr. Percy handed the bartender the money, choice A is incorrect because Mr. Percy handed over Frank's money. Choice B is incorrect because lunch was not completely free; he needed to buy a drink in order to get the free sandwiches. Choice

D is incorrect because nothing in the passage indicates that Frank wanted to spend time with Mr. Percy. Instead, paragraph 8 says that Frank was hungry.

20. D: Choice D is the best answer because Mr. Percy used Frank's money in order to get the drinks. Even though Mr. Percy claims that he'll pay Frank tomorrow, the reader can infer that he is probably lying. Choice C is incorrect because Mr. Percy tells Frank to be virtuous and happy as a way of dismissing Frank. However, he does not withhold the money because he feels that Frank is undeserving. Choice A is incorrect because Mr. Percy ordered drinks that he could not pay for with his own money. Although Mr. Percy says he'll be in the park, choice B is incorrect because Mr. Percy might be lying.

21. A: Choice A is the correct answer because Frank has realized that he has just lost all his money. The word *ruefully* shows that Frank is disappointed. Choice B is incorrect because Frank acted incautiously earlier in the passage when he gave Mr. Percy all his money. By paragraph 25, Frank is no longer incautious. Choice C is incorrect because Frank feels uneasy in paragraph 23. By paragraph 25, Frank realizes that Mr. Percy has cheated him. Choice D is incorrect because Frank is no longer suspicious about Mr. Percy's actions; he already knows that Mr. Percy is not going to repay him.

22. B: The best answer is choice B because both Andy and Frank experience a form of misfortune. Andy's misfortune is that his family has lost money and he can't return to school. Frank's misfortune is that he is all alone in the city and does not have any money. Choice A is incorrect because only Andy has a loving family; paragraph 25 of *The Telegraph Boy* shows that Frank is all alone. Choice C is incorrect because only Frank was tricked. Andy's family lost money because a banker stole it from his father. Choice D is incorrect because only *The Telegraph Boy* shows that Frank experiences hunger. *Andy Grant's Pluck* does not indicate that Andy will have trouble buying food.

23. C: The correct answer is choice C because Andy has no control over his family's finances, while Frank's poor decision to trust Mr. Percy led to his misfortune. Although *The Telegraph Boy* does not explain how Frank ended up alone with only twenty-five cents, choice A is incorrect because *The Telegraph Boy* does show how he ended up with no money at all. Choice B is incorrect because Andy is not all alone (he has his family); similarly, Frank does not have many friends (he is all alone). Choice D is incorrect because Andy was not tricked; instead, his father was robbed.

24. D: The correct answer is D because both selections end after the main characters have suffered misfortune. They don't know what the future holds for them. Choice A is incorrect because the characters have only experienced bad things; they are not feeling hopeful. Choice B is incorrect because Andy in *Andy Grant's Pluck* can't afford to go back to school. Furthermore, Frank in *The Telegraph Boy* never mentions school. Choice C is incorrect because the characters are not in immediate danger; they are uncertain about their future, but there are no threatening things around them.

25. C: The correct answer is choice C because the sentence shows that Andy feels disappointed, or the opposite of cheerful. Frank also feels disappointed after he loses all his money. Choice A is incorrect because the sentence simply describes Andy's father's problem; it does not show feelings. Choice B is incorrect because it shows Andy's determination to help his father; *The Telegraph Boy* does not have any moments where Frank shows determination. Choice D is incorrect because it is stating a fact rather than a feeling.

26. C: The correct answer is C because paragraph 2 says, "This new trouble concerns the building of the Nicaragua Canal." Choice A is incorrect because paragraph 5 says that people are looking for a way to avoid going around Cape Horn; sailors would be happy for a canal. Choice B is incorrect because the Panama Canal is an older, failed project. Paragraph D is incorrect because there is no canal called the Central America Canal. There are two possible canals that, if completed, would cut across Central America: the Nicaragua Canal and the Panama Canal.

27. B: The correct answer choice is B because paragraphs 15-19 detail the many financial problems that hurt the Panama Canal project. These problems include the dishonesty of several people involved in building the canal. Even though paragraph 15 mentions the Suez Canal, choice A is incorrect because the paragraph only mentions the Suez Canal to explain who Ferdinand de Lesseps is. Paragraph 18 does mention the French newspapers, but choice C is incorrect because paragraphs 15-19 are mostly about the problems that hurt the Panama Canal. While the bribing of the newspapers was one of the problems, it wasn't the entire one. Choice D is incorrect because the paragraphs don't go into detail about Ferdinand de Lesseps' time in jail; they only mention that he went to jail.

28. C: The correct answer is C because the sentence shows the dangers of going around Cape Horn. Choice A is incorrect because the sentence only discusses the way in which the Nicaragua Canal is affecting the treaty with Great Britain. Choice B is incorrect because it only details the location of Cape Horn without explaining why this location could encourage people to build a canal. Choice D is incorrect because it discusses steamships without explaining why a canal is needed.

29. A: The correct answer is A, informational, because the author includes many factual details about the Nicaragua and Panama Canals. Choice B is incorrect because the author strictly gives facts and does not include jokes that would make the passage humorous. Choice C is incorrect because the author doesn't withhold details that would add mystery to the passive. Choice D is incorrect because the author does not show emotions such as anger; he has an objective tone.

30. D: The passage explains in paragraph 23 that the Nicaragua Canal will go through existing waterways, which means that the builders will not have to cut through much land. Choice A is incorrect because, even though the Nicaragua Canal is longer, only 21 of those miles need to be cut through. This number contrasts with the 59 miles of the Panama Canal that needed to be cut through. Choice B is incorrect because the Panama Canal needed to be cut through the mountains, not the Nicaragua Canal. Choice C is incorrect because the passage does not say that the San Juan River is a canal. It simply says in paragraph 23 that the Nicaragua Canal will go through the San Juan River.

31. B: Although the passage does not give the date of the building of the Suez Canal, it does imply in paragraph 15 that the Suez Canal was built before the Panama and Nicaragua Canals when it says "the great Count Ferdinand de Lesseps, who built the Suez Canal." The passage also indicates that the Panama Canal was attempted before the Nicaragua Canal; the reason the Nicaragua Canal needed to be built was because the Panama Canal failed. Choices A, C, and D are incorrect because they do not show the correct chronological order.

32. D: The correct answer is D because the author is discussing the new plans for a canal, which will be the Nicaragua Canal. The author does this by giving some background of canals in Central America and describing details of the Nicaragua Canal. Choices A and B are incorrect because the author is very objective and does not argue for or against the Nicaragua Canal project; instead, he just gives information. Although the author does explain the problems that ended the Panama Canal project (in paragraph 15-20), this description is a small portion of the passage. The main purpose is to describe the issues surrounding the Nicaragua Canal.

33. A: The correct answer is A because blasting will create a long and deep cut in the in the earth. The first sentence of paragraph 22 says that a long and deep cut needed to be made. The next sentence says that this cut will be made by blasting. Choice B is incorrect because the phrase 'had to be made' doesn't give details about how blasting works. Choice C is incorrect because the phrase 'to build houses' talks about building something up rather than blasting something away. Choice D is incorrect because, while blasting may be long and tedious work, the phrase does not describe what blasting it is. It just describes the type of work that blasting is.

34. D: Choice D is the correct answer because paragraph 24 says that there is a volcano in Nicaragua Lake, which the canal will go through. Choice A is incorrect because Ferdinand de Lesseps and the other people in jail backed the Panama Canal, not the Nicaragua Canal. Choice B is incorrect because paragraph 22 shows that the Panama Canal, not the Nicaragua Canal, went through the mountains. Although paragraphs 1 and 2 say that the treaty may be defeated or delayed, this treaty is not a problem in building the canal. In contrast, the building of the canal affects the treaty.

35. C: The correct answer is C because the author wants to explain what happened in the past with the Panama Canal so readers can understand the history as well as possible problems with the Nicaragua Canal. Choice A is incorrect because the Panama Canal was never completed, which means it's not the other great canal in Central America. Choice B is incorrect because the author explains why the canal is needed in paragraphs 4-11. These paragraphs come before the discussion of the Panama Canal. Choice D is incorrect sailors still needed to go around Cape Horn because the Panama Canal was never completed. If the Nicaragua Canal is completed, the sailors will then be able to avoid Cape Horn.

36. A: The correct answer is A because the sentence discusses the people who, according to the passage, were not rich, but lost money on the Panama Canal. These people suffered the most because they fell into deeper poverty. Choice B is incorrect because the sentence shows who suffered but does not show the problems that caused the money loss. Choice C is incorrect because paragraph 19 says that people who were not rich are the people who lost the money. Choice D is incorrect because paragraph 20 says that the canal failed and that the project was not completed.

37. B: The correct answer is choice B because the passage explains that the only way for sailing vessels to get from the Atlantic Ocean to the Pacific Ocean is to go around Cape Horn. A canal will cut across Central America so that ships no longer need to go around Cape Horn. Choice A is incorrect because the canal will do the opposite by making sailing less dangerous. Choice C is incorrect because people needed to take the train before the canal was built. The train was the only way for people to go between shores while avoiding Cape Horn. Choice D is incorrect because the Panama Canal was planned to cut across at the narrowest point. The Nicaragua Canal would be 100 miles longer.

38. D: The correct answer is D because paragraph 19 says that he lived near Ettrick Water and that he was a keeper of sheep. Choice A is incorrect because he didn't get his nickname because he was Scottish; however, people all over Scotland knew who he was and called him the Ettrick Shepherd. Choices B and C are only partially correct. Both answers contributed to his nickname. Since choice D includes both, it is the best answer.

39. A: The passage says that the sheep scattered during the storm. James couldn't find them in the dark, although he did find them the next day. Choice B is incorrect because the passage does not say that Sirrah was scared; it says that the sheep were scared. Choice C is incorrect because paragraph 2 says that James sometimes watched several hundred sheep; he only had a problem with so many sheep when they became scared by the storm. Choice D is incorrect because the passage doesn't say that James got lost; instead, paragraph 6 says that he *lost sight* of the sheep. He knew where he was, but couldn't find the sheep.

40. B: The best answer is choice B because the poem describes several of the narrator's favorite places. The key word from the phrase is 'where'. The phrase is describing a specific place. Choice A is incorrect because the poem does not indicate that the narrator and Billy prefer blackbirds to other birds. Choice C is incorrect because the phrase "Where the blackbird sings the latest" is referring to the meadow. The next verse discusses the hay. Choice D is incorrect because the narrator doesn't say that the blackbird's song is his favorite song; he just mentions the song.

41. B: Choice B is correct because paragraph 13 says that James and the other shepherds counted the sheep to determine that they were all there. Choice A is incorrect because Sirrah is a dog and cannot speak. Choice C is incorrect because Sirrah rounded up the sheep, not James. Choice D is incorrect because the passage does not say he was the best shepherd; in fact, the passage does not describe the quality of his skills at all.

42. A: The correct answer is A because the poem shows a sense of wonder and excitement. The last verse also says, "I love to play", which shows how much the narrator likes to play and have fun. Choice B is incorrect because the narrator does not show fear. Instead, he shows an enthusiasm for life. Choice C is incorrect because the poem shows a lot of curiosity; the narrator describes all his favorite places and may be curious about them. Choice D is incorrect because the narrator demonstrates his love of exploring when he describes all the details of the meadow, the hay, the water, and the lea.

43. B: The correct answer is B because paragraph 6 says that James started searching for the sheep once he realized they were gone. Choice A is incorrect because the selection does not indicate that James wrote a poem immediately after losing the sheep. Furthermore, the poem in the passage is not about the sheep. Choice C is incorrect because James always lived in Scotland; the answer choice is not an event that happened after he lost the sheep. While it's true that Sirrah gathered up the sheep, choice D is incorrect because it happened after James searched for the sheep.

44. C: The correct answer is choice C because paragraph 2 says that it was his business to take care of the sheep, which means that it was his job. Choice A is incorrect because the passage shows that being a shepherd is his business. He makes money from doing it, which means he's not doing a favor. Choice B is incorrect for the same reason; James may like the sheep, but he takes care of them to earn money. Choice D is also incorrect; while James liked Sirrah and says in paragraph 16 that he is grateful to him, James is a shepherd because it's his family's business.

45. B: The correct answer is B. The passage says that he read through the prose, which implies that the prose is a form of writing. While the prose is in a book, choice A is incorrect because the word 'volume' is referring to the book. Choice C is incorrect because the paragraph says that no libraries were near James Hogg. When he wanted a book of prose, he needed to buy or borrow it. Choice D is incorrect because he may have learned from the book, but 'prose' does not mean to learn. It is a noun that means a type of writing.

46. A: The correct answer is A because the narrator frequently mentions doing things with Billy. The phrase "That's the way for Billy and me" shows that the narrator and Billy probably spend a lot of time together and are friends. Choice B is incorrect because the poem does not refer to being a shepherd at all. While the poem expresses the narrator's loves nature, the repeated mention of Billy at the end of each verse emphasizes the close friendship between the narrator and Billy. Choice D is incorrect because the poem indicates that Billy and the narrator are friends. Although the third verse mentions fighting, it does not refer to fighting with Billy.

47. C: It is clear from paragraph 7 that James and the other shepherds are looking for the sheep. The second sentence of paragraph 8 also shows that they are looking for the sheep. Choice A is incorrect because 'sought' means to look for something, not to see something, as shown in paragraphs 7 and 8. While the word *sought* rhymes with *thought*, it means to seek or look for something, as indicated by the second sentence of the paragraph. Choice D is incorrect because James and the shepherds are looking for the sheep.

48. A: James felt surprised because Sirrah managed to gather all the sheep; the selection says he's surprised in paragraph 13. Choice B is incorrect because, while James might have been scared during the storm, he was relieved when he found the sheep. While James might have felt tired after staying up all night, choice A is a better answer than choice C because the passage says that he and the shepherds were surprised. Choice D is incorrect because James had no reason to be disappointed; he found the sheep he thought he had lost and was happy.

Written Expression

1. B: In Paragraph 2, "dominates" means "takes over." The author is using the word to show how much of the small room is taken up by the large table.

2. A: "Desperate" is the best choice because to describe Mandie's feelings in the beginning of the play about being left alone with Mammie. She is clinging to her husband and begging him not to leave her alone with his mother.

3. C: Paragraph 5 clearly shows Anthony's dismissive attitude when he calls Mandie "silly."

4. D: The "Characters" section of this play (Paragraph 1) describes Mammie as Anthony's mother.

5. C: Silence and action contribute to the development of Mammie's character by showing how awkwardly she relates to Mandie.

6. D: Paragraph 24 clearly shows Mammie's critical tendencies in the way she responds to Mandie's ignorance, when she tells her to stop being silly, because everyone knows how to cook rice.

7. B: Paragraph 4 shows Mandie's feelings about Mammie when she says, "She doesn't like me."

8. C: Mandie's relationship with Mammie begins to improve when Mammie tells Mandy that when Anthony was growing up, he loved to stick his finger into the middle brownie after she baked them, and Mandy replies by laughing about the fact that he still does it.

9. A: is The most important lesson of this short play is that people can get along with each other better when they share common interests or experiences.

10. D: The fact that the kitchen is small and cramped doesn't have much of a bearing on the story at all, but the other three answer choices represent important points in the play.

Mometrix

11. B is the correct answer because it is an expression of a person's view of the play, using the words "powerful" and "poignant," making it an opinion. A summary gives a factual description of a play, while an opinion is one person's unique take on it.

12. A: When Mandie says "*we* have work to do", it illustrates the newfound camaraderie between herself and Mammie.

13. A: The word "passé" means "outdated."

14. D: The three key benefits discussed in this article are health benefits, financial benefits, and environmental benefits.

15. B: Paragraph 1 indicates that the author has been a vegetarian for a decade, which is 10 years.

16. D: In paragraph 3, the vegetarian lifestyle is compared to a weapon.

17. A: This article is written in first-person point of view.

18. C: The author's perspective is that being a vegetarian offers many benefits, but we know she doesn't feel that "it's the only way to go", because she says that she never pressures her friends to become vegetarians.

19. C: Paragraph 2 indicates that the author needs 50 grams of protein each day.

20. B: In Paragraph 1, when the author says, "Mom just nodded and smiled knowingly", she follows it up in the next sentence by stating that her mother was assuming that vegetarianism was just going to another of the author's many phases.

21. B: A controlling idea is an idea that represents one of the main points the author is making. One of her main points is that being a vegetarian improves one's finances. She makes the other points, too, but they are subordinate to her overall main points.

22. C is the only answer choice that is a personal opinion of this article, rather than a fact-based description of it.

23. A best represents the author's main objective in this article, which is to show people the benefits of vegetarianism that they may not be aware of. She is certainly not trying to force anyone to become a vegetarian. She does discuss the ill effects of factory farms and eating meat on animals and the environment, but they are minor points, not her main one.

24. D: Paragraph 8 best encapsulates both the main ideas and purpose of the article. As it's the final paragraph in the piece, this should come as no surprise, because many authors of short articles such as this one will use their final paragraph to recap and summarize the whole.

25. A: is the best choice because the best definition of "sacrilegious" as it appears in paragraph 2 is "absurdly inappropriate." This is not the literal meaning of "sacreligious", which means "not showing proper respect to something holy." The author is using the word figuratively, to say that going inside would be a complete waste of the nice weather, and completely out of place because of all the activity that had taken place outdoors that day.

26. C: Will's attitude in Paragraph 15 is best described as sentimental, because he's expressing strong emotions.

27. B: Personification is used to describe the stars in Paragraph 11, when the author says the stars "winked." Winking is something that human beings do, and personification is attributing a human trait or actions to something that isn't human.

28. A best illustrates how Puck's death is an example of irony, which is when something happens in a way that's the opposite of what one would expect.

29. D is the only option that is a main idea in this story. The other three answer selections are all supporting ideas, not main ideas in the story.

30. B: "Pallor" means "paleness."

31. D: This essay is best classified as a memoir, or a personal recollection by a writer.

32. A: The main purpose of this piece is to honor and say goodbye to Grandfather. The other answer choices represent aspects of the piece, but none of them are the main reason the author had in mind for writing this.

33. C: The author uses repetition in this piece to increase its power and impact. Every paragraph but the last begins with the phrase "I will always remember my grandfather", which is followed by a snapshot of what he was like at that point in his life.

34. C: Being fed with a syringe is the image that most strongly illustrates Grandfather's powerlessness, because being unable to feed one's self is a state of extreme weakness. The other answer choices represent age-related problems, but not powerlessness.

35. A: The common theme that most unites these passages is loss of a loved one. This is not to imply that the loss of a dog is equivalent to the loss of a grandparent, but only that both pieces are about deeply felt personal loss.

36. B: The first piece is written in third-person point of view and the second is in first-person point of view.

37. C: The reason the grief in "Puck" seems more vivid is because it comes as a sudden shock, whereas in the other piece, the grandfather's decline takes place over years, and is the natural process most people will experience as they age.

38. B: Both paragraphs express reminiscence in the face of loss.

39. D: Charles schulz should be changed to Charles Schulz.

40. B: Sentence 5 functions as the thesis statement for this composition. It briefly tells the reader what he'll learn in the piece, in much more depth. It reveals the author's main points.

41. A: Changing "inert" to "inept" corrects the meaning of sentence, because inert is not the correct word choice here. It means motionless, unable to move, barely moving, etc., while "inept" means unskilled. It's much more likely that the author meant to say that Charles Schulz was unskilled at sports, rather than saying that he just stood motionless while engaged in athletic endeavors.

42. C: Sentence 10 is a comma splice with two independent clauses, which is incorrect. Two independent clauses should be joined by a semicolon, not a comma.

43. A: Swapping sentences 13 and 14 will improve the organization and flow of paragraph 3, because they are out of chronological order as written. This is jarring and confusing to the reader.

44. C: The word "appreciated" is a misspelling; the correct spelling is "appreciated."

45. B: A colon is the correct punctuation in sentence 17, not a semicolon.

46. A: Sentence 18 is correct as written.

47. D: The author has been talking about Sparky's struggles to succeed, and the history of the Peanuts strip, and in the final paragraph he demonstrates just how successful Sparky became, all thanks to the popularity of Peanuts. Sentence 21 serves as a transitional sentence between these two aspects of the article.

48. B: The word "appeared" is the correct word to replace the misused word "appointed."

49. B: The word "stiffling" is a misspelling; it should be "stifling".

50. C: Sentence 5 functions as the thesis statement for this essay. It's a brief summation of what the author intends to demonstrate in the entire article. Demonstrating that summer is the best season by giving three reasons is the author's main purpose in writing this piece.

51. D: In normal usage, the names of the seasons should not be capitalized, so "Summer" should be "summer."

52. A is correct because both verbs are now in the present tense. As written, the first verb in the sentence, "were" is in past tense, while the second verb, "roll", is in present tense. This is unacceptable. The article is written using the present tense for every other verb, so both verbs in this sentence should also be in present tense.

53. B: The word "simpler" is the correct comparative form of "simple." The phrase "more simple" would also be acceptable here, in order to match the construction of "more relaxed", but "more simpler" is never acceptable.

54. A: No change is necessary; sentence 11 is correct as written.

55. B: The word "hamocks" is a misspelling; it should be "hammocks."

56. D: A comma should follow the word "relaxation" in order to separate the introductory phrase from the main clause of the sentence.

57. C: Sentence 22 is written with passive construction, which is very awkward sounding. It should be written in the active voice: "I love the long, lazy, school-free days."

58. A: Sentence 25 is correct as written.

Mathematics

1. A: The numbers listed for Choice A can all be converted to decimal form for comparison. The given sequence can be written as $-2, -0.75, -0.45, 0.03, 0.36$. The negative integers are the least values, with the negative integer with the greatest absolute value, serving as the least integer. The percentage, 3%, is written as 0.03, and is less than 0.36.

M⊘metrix

2. B: The sequence can be converted to decimals and written as 0.875, 0.8, 0.5, −3, −8. The hundredths place can be used to compare the first two decimals, while the tenths place can be used to compare all three decimals. The negative integers are smallest when the absolute value is greatest. Thus, the sequence for Choice B is written in order from greatest to least.

3. C: Dilation of the pentagon by a scale factor of one-third indicates that each dimension of the dilated figure will be one-third that of the dimension in the original figure. Thus, the measurements of the dilated figure can be written as: $9 \cdot \frac{1}{3}$ cm, or 3 cm; $18 \cdot \frac{1}{3}$ cm, or 6 cm; $24 \cdot \frac{1}{3}$ cm, or 8 cm; $18 \cdot \frac{1}{3}$ cm, or 6 cm; and $9 \cdot \frac{1}{3}$ cm, or 3 cm.

4. C: The circumference of a circle can be found by using the formula, $C = \pi d$. Since the radius is equal to 3 inches, the diameter is equal to 6 inches. Substituting a value of 6 inches for d and estimating pi to be 3, gives an approximate circumference of 18 inches.

5. B: In order to find the number of whole pizzas eaten in 5 weeks, the amount of pizza eaten each week $\left(\frac{5}{6}\right)$ should be multiplied by the total number of weeks (5); $\frac{5}{6} \cdot 5 = \frac{25}{6}$, which is slightly more than 4 pizzas.

6. B: The value, recorded as 2.71×10^4, can be written as 27,100 by moving the decimal point 4 places to the right. Thus, the cruising altitude is 27,100 feet.

7. A: The slope is $0.25, and the y-intercept is –$18, so the correct steps for finding the profit after selling 49 cookies, will include multiplication of the slope, $0.25, by the number of cookies, 49, and adding the expenses, or y-intercept, of –18. Thus, you must multiply 49 by $0.25 and subtract $18, in order to find the profit.

8. C: One-fifth of $1,000 is $200; a donation of $30 per charity results in a total of $240 in donations. This amount is more than his allotted one-fifth of savings. Thus, the estimate is not reasonable.

9. B: Since 7 feet equals 84 inches, and 1 inch equals 2.54 centimeters. The proportion can be written as: $\frac{84}{x} = \frac{1}{2.54}$. Solving for x gives: $x = 213.36$. Thus, the bed is 213.36 centimeters in length.

10. C: The proportion can be written as: $\frac{4.85}{7.3} = \frac{x}{5}$. Solving for x gives: $7.3x = 24.25$, or $x = 3.32$. Thus, the cost of 5 ounces of lotion is approximately $3.32.

11. D: The number of miles Kevin drives per hour can be written as $y = 65x$, where x represents the number of hours and y represents the total number of miles driven. The y-intercept is 0, since there is not an amount added to, or subtracted from, this term. The graph of the line passes through the origin, or the point, $(0, 0)$.

12. D: The table shown for Choice D is arithmetic, but does not have a y-intercept of 0. The y-intercept is 3. Therefore, Store D does not report a proportional relationship.

13. C: A graph that has a y-intercept of 0 indicates a proportional relationship because the starting value is 0, and no amount is added to, or subtracted from, the term, containing the slope.

14. C: In order to find the amount of savings, the original vehicle price must be multiplied by the discount percentage of 15%; $39,500 \cdot 0.15 = $5,925.

110

Copyright © Mometrix Media. You have been licensed one copy of this document for personal use only. Any other reproduction or redistribution is strictly prohibited. All rights reserved.
This content is provided for test preparation purposes only and does not imply an endorsement by Mometrix of any particular political, scientific, or religious point of view.

15. A: The proportion can be written as: $\frac{2}{80} = \frac{50}{x}$. Solving for x gives: $2x = 4,000$, or $x = 2,000$.

16. C: Since the triangles are similar, $\overline{AB} = \overline{DE}$ and $\overline{AC} = \overline{DF}$. Thus, The proportion can be written as: $\frac{18}{27} = \frac{11}{x}$. Solving for x gives: $18x = 297$, or $x = 16.5$. Thus, $\overline{DF}$ is 16.5 inches, in length.

17. D: The table represents the equation, $y = 9x - 4$. The slope can be determined by calculating the ratio of the change in two y-values to the change in two corresponding x-values. For example, $\frac{-13-(-31)}{-1-(-3)} = \frac{18}{2}$, or 9. Thus, the slope is equal to 9. The y-intercept is the value of y, when x is equal to 0; thus, the table reveals the y-intercept to be −4. The graph for Choice D has a y-intercept of −4 and a slope of 9. The slope can be found by choosing any two points and calculating the ratio of the change in y-value to the change in x-value.

18. D: Since she earns $2,500 each month, this amount represents the y-intercept, or the constant amount added each month. Earnings of 5% of each insurance premium sale are variable, depending on the value of the earnings; thus this amount represents the slope. The total amount earned can be represented by the equation, $y = 0.05x + 2500$.

19. C: The table has a slope of −3; $\frac{-4-5}{1-(-2)} = \frac{-9}{3}$, or −3. The y-intercept is the value of y, when x is equal to 0. Thus, 3 can be added to −4, in order to determine the y-intercept. The y-intercept is −1. The value of the slope and the x- and y-values from an ordered pair can also be substituted into the slope-intercept form of an equation, in order to determine the y-intercept.

20. A: The graph has a y-intercept of −7 and a slope of 12. The slope can be determined by writing the following ratio: $\frac{-7-5}{0-1}$, which equals 12.

21. C: The initial deposit of $245 represents the constant amount, or y-intercept. The recurring deposits of $125 per month represent the slope of the variable amount. Thus, the equation, $y = 125x + 245$, can be used to find the amount in savings, after x months. Five years equals 60 months, and substitution of 60 for the variable, x, gives: $y = 125(60) + 245$, or 7,745. Thus, Hannah will have $7,745 in her account after 5 years.

22. C: In order to find the 46th term in the sequence, 46 should be substituted for the variable, x, in the equation, $y = 6x - 8$. Doing so gives: $y = 6(46) - 8$, or $y = 268$. Thus, the 46th term is 268.

23. B: The slope of the sequence can be determined by assigning the term numbers 1, 2, 3, 4, and so on, to each value in the sequence, namely, $-3, -8, -13, -18, \ldots$ Therefore, the slope can be calculated by writing the ratio of the change in any two term values to the change in any two term numbers; $\frac{-8-(-3)}{2-1} = \frac{-5}{1} = -5$. The slope of −5 and the x- and y-values from the point, $(1, -3)$ can be substituted into the equation, $y = mx + b$, in order to determine the y-intercept; $-3 = -5(1) + b$, or $b = 2$. Thus the equation, $y = -5x + 2$, represents the given sequence. Substitution of the value, 21, for the variable, x, gives: $y = -5(21) + 2$, or $y = -103$. Thus, the 21st term in the sequence is −103.

24. C: The dilated triangle has dimensions equal to $\frac{3}{4}$ of the dimensions in the original triangle. Thus, the dimensions in the dilated triangle can be written as: $9 \cdot \frac{3}{4}$ cm, or 6.75 cm; $4 \cdot \frac{3}{4}$ cm, or 3 cm, and $7 \cdot \frac{3}{4}$ cm, or 5.25 cm.

25. B: The width of the enlarged rectangle is equal to the product of 9 in and $\frac{3}{2}$, or 13.5 in. The length of the enlarged rectangle is equal to the product of 15 in and $\frac{3}{2}$, or 22.5 in. $Perimeter_{rectangle} = 2w + 2l$. Thus, the perimeter is equal to 2×13.5 in $+ 2 \times 22.5$ in $= 72$ in.

26. A: The reflection of a figure about the x-axis requires the negation of the y-value. The vertices of the given triangle are $(3, 9)$, $(2, 4)$, and $(6, 2)$. Thus, the vertices of the triangle, reflected about the x-axis, are $(3, -9)$, $(2, -4)$, and $(6, -2)$.

27. D: The vertices of the given trapezoid are $(-5, 2)$, $(-2, 4)$, $(2, 4)$, and $(5, 2)$. A shift of 8 units to the left and 4 units up is indicated by $(x - 8, y + 4)$. Thus, the vertices of the translated trapezoid are $(-13, 6)$, $(-10, 8)$, $(-6, 8)$, and $(-3, 6)$.

28. B: The triangle has side lengths of 18 inches, 9 inches, and 11 inches. An enlargement by a scale factor of 4 requires multiplication of each original side length by 4; $18 \cdot 4 = 72$; $9 \cdot 4 = 36$; and $11 \cdot 4 = 44$. Thus, the enlarged triangle has side lengths of 72 inches, 36 inches, and 44 inches.

29. C: The figure is a square pyramid because it has a square base and four triangular faces.

30. D: The ordered pair, represented by Point P, is $(4, -9)$ because the corresponding x-value is 4, and the corresponding y-value is -9.

31. D: The figure is a triangular pyramid because it has a triangular base and three triangular faces.

32. C: The lateral surface area of a triangular prism is equal to the sum of the areas of the three rectangular faces. The area of each rectangular face is equal to the product of 12 cm and 15 cm, or 180 cm^2; the total lateral surface area is equal to the product of 3 and 180 cm^2, or 540 cm^2.

33. B: The surface area of a square pyramid can be determined by using the formula, $A = s^2 + 2sl$, where s represents the length of each side of the square base and l represents the slant height. Substituting a square side length of 4 inches and a slant height of 9 inches gives: $A = 4^2 + 2(4)(9)$, or 88. Thus, the surface area of the square pyramid is 88 in^2.

34. C: The number of cubic inches of space available inside the box is represented by the volume of the box. The volume of a rectangular prism can be determined by calculating the product of the length, width, and height. Doing so gives: $18 \cdot 9 \cdot 6$, or 972. Thus, there are 972 cubic inches of space available inside the box.

35. B: The lateral surface area of a cylinder can be determined by evaluating the expression, $2\pi rh$, where r represents the radius and h represents the height of the cylinder. Substituting the radius of 8 inches and the height of 14 inches allows you to write: $2\pi(8)(14)$, which is approximately 703.36. Thus, the lateral surface area of the cylinder is approximately 703.36 square inches.

36. A: The volume of a cone can be found by using the formula, $V = \frac{1}{3}\pi r^2 h$.

37. C: The amount of wrapping paper she will need is equal to the surface area of the box. The surface area of a rectangular prism can be determined by using the formula: $SA = 2(lw) + 2(lh) = 2(wh)$. Substituting the given dimensions allows you to write: $SA = 2(22 \cdot 19) + 2(22 \cdot 17) + 2(19 \cdot 17)$, which equals 2,230. Thus, she will need 2,230 square inches of wrapping paper.

38. A: The base of a triangular pyramid is a triangle. Thus, the area of the base is equal to $\frac{1}{2}bh$.

Mömetrix

39. A: The volume of a sphere is represented by the equation, $V = \frac{4}{3}\pi r^3$.

40. B: The area of the lateral face of a cylinder is calculated by using the expression, $2\pi rh$, where r represents the radius and h represents the height. Substitution of the radius of 6 inches and height of 8 inches into the formula gives: $2\pi(6)(8)$, or 96π. Thus, he will paint 96π square inches.

41. C: The distance from his home to the park can be determined by using the Pythagorean Theorem, or $a^2 + b^2 = c^2$; $0.5^2 + 1^2 = c^2$; $c \approx 1.1$. Therefore, the distance from Oliver's home to the park is approximately 1.1 miles.

42. A: The possible dimensions for a right triangle with an area of 28 square centimeters are 7 cm and 8 cm; 14 cm and 4 cm; or 28 cm and 2 cm. The dimensions of 14 cm and 16 cm are twice that of a right triangle with dimensions of 7 cm and 8 cm.

43. C: A square with side length, a, has an area equal to s^2. A square with side length of $6a$ has an area equal to $36a^2$. Thus, the area of the second square is 36 times larger.

44. B: A cylinder with a height of 9 inches and radius of 4 inches has a volume equal to $\pi(4)^2(9)$ cubic inches, or approximately 452.16 cubic inches. A cylinder with a height of 9 inches and a radius of 12 inches has a volume equal to $\pi(12)^2(9)$ cubic inches, or approximately 4,069.44 cubic inches. The volume of the second cylinder is 9 times larger than the volume of the original cylinder.

45. C: The probability of independent events, A and B, can be found, by using the formula, $P(A \text{ and } B) = P(A) \cdot P(B)$. Thus, the probability can be written as $\frac{1}{2} \cdot \frac{4}{52}$, or $\frac{4}{104}$, which reduces to $\frac{1}{26}$.

46. C: The probability of independent events, A or B, can be found, by using the formula, (A or B) = P(A) + P(B) - P(A-B). Thus, the probability can be written as 3/6 + 1/2 - 1/4, or 3/4.

47. D: The probability of independent events, A or B, can be found, by using the formula, $P(A \text{ or } B) = P(A) + P(B)$. Thus, the probability can be written as $\frac{3}{6} + \frac{1}{6}$, or $\frac{4}{6}$, which reduces to $\frac{2}{3}$.

48. B: The probability of dependent events, A and B, can be found, by using the formula, $P(A \text{ or } B) = P(A) + P(B) - P(A \text{ and } B)$. Thus, the probability can be written as $\frac{3}{6} + \frac{4}{6} - \frac{2}{6}$, or $\frac{5}{6}$.

49. B: The theoretical probability of rolling a number greater than 4 is $\frac{2}{6}$. The most accurate prediction for the number of times he will roll a number greater than 4, out of 18 rolls, is equal to the product of 18 and $\frac{1}{3}$, or 6.

50. B: The outlier of 13 will skew the data. The mean and range will be significantly impacted. Therefore, the median is the most appropriate measure for reflecting the number of houses she sold per year. This data set does not have a mode and is thus not the most appropriate.

51. D: A box-and-whiskers plot identifies the median, as part of the graphical representation. The median, Q2, as well as the median of the lower quartile, Q1, and the median of the upper quartile, Q3, are identified.

52. C: A line graph can be used to track data over a period of time.

53. D: The smallest negative integers are those that have the largest absolute value. Therefore, the negative integers, written in order from least to greatest, are $-8, -7\frac{4}{5}, -\frac{3}{4}$. The percent, 18%, can

113

Copyright © Mometrix Media. You have been licensed one copy of this document for personal use only. Any other reproduction or redistribution is strictly prohibited. All rights reserved.
This content is provided for test preparation purposes only and does not imply an endorsement by Mometrix of any particular political, scientific, or religious point of view.

be written as the decimal, 0.18; 0.18 is less than 0.25. The decimal, 2.5, is the greatest rational number given. Thus, the values, $-8, -7\frac{4}{5}, -\frac{3}{4}, 18\%, 0.25, 2.5$, are written in order from least to greatest.

54. B: The fraction, $2\frac{1}{4}$, can be written as the decimal, 2.25. The fraction, $2\frac{2}{5}$, can be written as the decimal, 2.40. The fraction, $2\frac{3}{8}$, can be written as the decimal, 2.375; 2.375 is larger than 2.25 but smaller than 2.40.

55. D: The length of Rectangle B can be determined by writing the following proportion: $\frac{18}{4} = \frac{x}{6}$. Solving for x gives $x = 27$. Thus, the length of Rectangle B is 27 cm.

56. B: The Pythagorean Theorem, $a^2 + b^2 = c^2$, can be used to find the length of the hypotenuse. Substituting the given measurements for the base and height, the following equation can be written: $9^2 + 8^2 = c^2$. Solving for c gives $145 = c^2$, or $c = \sqrt{145}$, which is approximately 12.04. Thus, the length of the hypotenuse is approximately 12.04 inches.

57. A: Since a square has four equal side lengths, the given perimeter can be divided by 4, in order to determine the length of each side; 5.66 ÷ 4 = 1.415, which is the approximate value of $\sqrt{2}$. Squaring the value of one side gives the area to be approximately 2 cm².

58. D: The number, 0.0095, can be written in scientific notation by moving the decimal point behind the 9 and counting the number of places the decimal was moved. Since the decimal point was moved 3 places, the number can be written as 9.5×10^{-3}. The exponent is negative because the decimal point must be moved three places to the left, in order to get back to the original decimal number.

59. C: The distance, in miles, given by 5.9×10^9, indicates that the number will be larger than 5.9, since the decimal point will be moved 9 places to the right. The number of miles Pluto is from the sun is thus 5,900,000,000, since 8 zeros must be added to the number.

60. D: The amount Aisha invests doubles each month. Thus, the invested amounts for months 1 – 6 are as follows: $26.25, $52.50, $105, $210, $420, and $840. She invests $840 during the sixth month.

61. A: The amount Jackson donates can be written as $\frac{1}{2}a - 3$, where a represents the amount Amy donates. Substituting 128 for a gives $\frac{1}{2}(128) - 3$, which equals 64 – 3, or 61. Thus, Jackson donates $61.

62. C: The number of miles Lauren must drive can be rounded to 1,500; 1,500 miles divided by 5 days equals 300 miles per day. Thus, a reasonable estimate for the number of miles driven per day is 300.

63. C: Since 1 foot equals 0.3048 meters, The proportion can be written as: $\frac{1}{0.3048} = \frac{12}{x}$. Solving for x gives $x = 3.6576$, which rounds to 3.66. Thus, the length of the bridge is approximately 3.66 meters.

64. C: The table for Choice C represents the proportional equation, $y = 6x$. A proportion is represented by the equation, $y = kx$, where k represents some constant multiplier. In a proportion, the graph of the equation passes through the point, (0, 0), indicating a y-intercept of 0. In other words, the equation does not have a value added to or subtracted from the expression, kx.

65. D: The equation, $y = 2x + 8$, is not proportional because the graph of the line does not pass through the origin, (0, 0). In other words, a value, other than 0, is added to the expression, $2x$. A proportional equation is represented as $y = kx$.

66. A: The graph for Choice A passes through the origin, (0, 0), indicating a proportional relationship.

67. D: The discount is equal to the product of the original price, $328, and the percentage of the discount, 0.15; $328 × 0.15 = $49.20. Thus, the amount of the discount is equal to $49.20.

68. C: The following proportion can be used to solve the problem: $\frac{10}{3} = \frac{x}{30}$. Solving for x gives: $x = 100$. Thus, the professor would submit 100 articles, according to the trend.

69. B: The following proportion can be used to solve the problem: $\frac{56}{4} = \frac{x}{30}$. Solving for x gives: $x = 420$. Thus, she consumes 420 grams of protein in 30 days.

70. C: The value of the 18th term can be found by substituting 18 for the variable, x, in the equation, $y = 6x + 2$. Doing so gives: $y = 6(18) + 2$, or $y = 110$. Therefore, the value of the 18th term is 110.

71. A: The amount of money he has already saved represents the y-intercept. The amount of money he intends to save per month represents the slope. Thus, his savings can be represented by the equation, $y = 28x + 15$, also written as $y = 15 + 28x$.

72. D: The graph for Choice D reveals a negative slope, with the y-values decreasing as the x-values increase. The slope is indeed –8. The graph for Choice D also reveals a y-intercept of 8, with the graph crossing the y-axis at the point (0, 8).

73. B: In order to determine the number of parking spaces painted per hour, the slope for the change in number of spaces painted per change in number of hours taken needs to be calculated. Substituting the values, 91 and 52, for the number of spaces painted, and 7 and 4, for the number of hours taken, gives the following ratio: $\frac{91-52}{7-4}$, which equals 13. Thus, 13 parking spaces are painted per hour.

74. A: The cost of the monthly service can be represented by the equation, $y = 0.07x + 12$, where x represents the number of text messages sent and y represents the total cost of the bill. The cost for sending 0 text messages is $12, e.g., $y = 0.07(0) + 12$. The cost for sending 1 text messages is $12.07, e.g., $y = 0.07(1) + 12$. The change in y-values per change in x-values is 0.07, with a y-intercept or initial cost of $12. The table for Choice A represents the correct slope and y-intercept.

75. C: According to the given translation specifications, the x-value will be shifted 3 units left, represented by the expression, $x - 3$, while the y-value will be shifted up 6 units, represented by the expression, $y + 6$. The ordered pairs, representing the vertices of the translated triangle can be determined by writing: A′(2 – 3, 8 + 6), B′(4 – 3, 8 + 6), C′(3 – 3, 12 + 6). Thus, the vertices of the translated triangle can be written as: A′(−1, 14), B′(1, 14), and C′(0, 18).

Science

1. B: The *reactants* are the chemicals that react to produce the products. They always appear on the left-hand side of the chemical equation. In this case, the reactants are $C_{12}H_{12}O_{11}$ (sucrose) and O_2 (molecular oxygen).

2. A: An *exothermic* reaction produces energy; an *endothermic* reaction absorbs energy. Because energy appears as a product on the right-hand side of the equation, this reaction is exothermic.

3. B: According to the coefficients in this equation, for every molecule of sucrose and every twelve molecules of oxygen among the reactants, eleven molecules of water are produced. Therefore, if five molecules of sucrose react with sixty (twelve times five) molecules of oxygen, they will produce fifty-five (eleven times five) molecules of water.

4. D: The *troposphere* is the layer of the atmosphere closest to Earth, where most clouds form and other weather phenomena occur. Above the troposphere is the stratosphere, then the mesosphere, and then the thermosphere; beyond even that is the exosphere, which fades into outer space. (Some systems also mention the *ionosphere*, where phenomena such as the aurora borealis occur, but most scientists consider that part of the thermosphere.)

5. B: Atmospheric pressure decreases with altitude; the atmospheric pressure is greater at lower altitudes because of the weight of the atmosphere above pressing down.

6. C: Both the fungus and the alga benefit from the relationship. Such a relationship is known as *mutualism*. In *commensalism,* one organism benefits, while the other is not significantly affected, while in *parasitism*, one organism benefits at the expense of the other. *Competition* refers to two organisms vying for the same resource and does not apply to this situation.

7. C: The sound's volume, or *amplitude,* corresponds to the vertical distance covered by the wave function. The sound's pitch, or *frequency,* corresponds to the horizontal distance covered by a single oscillation (cycle). The question states the sound varies in volume (amplitude) but not in frequency. Choice A has a constant volume and frequency. Choice B varies in frequency but not in volume—the width of the oscillations varies but not their height. Choice D varies in both volume and frequency. Only Choice C shows a waveform that varies in volume but not in frequency—the oscillations have different heights but constant width.

8. A: The *beat frequency* is the difference between the lower and higher notes. Lowering the higher note would put the two notes closer together, therefore decreasing their difference. Raising the higher note would have the opposite effect, while lowering or raising both notes by the same amount would have no effect on the beat frequency.

9. C: Seasons occur because of the tilt of the Earth's axis; as one hemisphere is tilted toward the Sun that hemisphere experiences summer, while the other hemisphere, tilted away from the Sun, experiences winter. The tides occur because of the gravitational pull of the moon, and day and night occur because of the Earth's rotation; neither of those phenomena depends on the tilt of the Earth's axis.

10. C: Mercury is closer to the Sun than the Earth, so a planet closer than Mercury would be even closer. A planet that close to the Sun would be much hotter than the Earth; in general, the closer to the Sun, the hotter. Nothing definitive could be said about the (hypothetical) planet's density; Mercury is less dense than Earth, but only slightly, and there's no obvious reason a planet closer to the Sun couldn't be denser.

11. D: The function of the Golgi apparatus is to package proteins that are to be sent to their destinations elsewhere in the cell. The proteins are actually synthesized by ribosomes at the endoplasmic reticulum. The mitochondria produce energy for the cell, while the cell membrane serves at the cell's boundary.

12. D: Mitosis is the process by which a cell splits into two daughter cells. In the first stage of mitosis, called *prophase,* the cell's DNA condenses into compact chromosomes; in the next stage, *metaphase,* the chromosomes align along a plane; in *anaphase,* the chromosomes are pulled apart to opposite ends of the cell; and in the last phase, *telophase,* the nuclear membranes reform about the separated chromosomes, ready to form the nuclei of the two new cells. A cell with two separate sets of chromosomes is in either anaphase or telophase.

13. B: Different cells have different shapes to match their functions. A nerve cell has a long axon with which it connects to other nerve cells and branching dendrites where other nerve cells connect to it. The cell pictured fits that description; the axon is the long projection to the right. Muscle cells are elongated, tapering at both ends. Red blood cells are flat, concave disks. White blood cells are blob shaped.

14. A: A *compound* consists of a single substance (molecule), with more than one chemical element. Water (H_2O) is one example of a compound; it contains two elements: hydrogen and water. A *mixture* is a combination of two or more different substances (compounds); it is *homogeneous* if they are evenly mixed and *heterogeneous* otherwise. A *solution* is a homogeneous mixture in which the two substances are thoroughly mixed at the molecular level.

15. D: Copper, gold, and iron all appear on the periodic table as elements 29, 79, and 26, respectively (chemical symbols Cu, Au, and Fe). Steel does not appear on the periodic table. It is in fact a mixture of several different elements, mostly iron but with some carbon (element 6, C) and possibly some other elements as well. The added carbon makes the steel stronger than pure iron but less flexible.

16. D: Igneous rocks are formed by molten rock refreezing and becoming solid. Most igneous rocks form deep beneath the Earth's surface, where the temperature is great enough to melt rock. However, molten rock also comes out of volcanoes in the form of lava, and this too can solidify into igneous rock. Atolls (which are formed from coral), mountaintops, and riverbeds do not generally include molten rock, so igneous rocks will not form there.

17. A: Examining the data, it's clear that the number of large-mandibled beetles is increasing. This is likely because they have some survival advantage that allows them to have a greater chance to pass on their genes to their offspring. While Choice B may seem plausible, it doesn't explain why there weren't already more large-mandibled beetles in the wild population. Choice A is the best explanation for the given data.

18. D: By the process of natural selection, individuals with an advantageous trait are more likely to survive to pass on that trait to their offspring. This is true regardless of whether the trait in question happens to be dominant or recessive.

19. D: A *population* is a group of individuals of the same species that live in a particular area. A *community* comprises all the populations in an area and includes multiple species. An *ecosystem* also includes abiotic factors such as water and air, and a *biome* is a set of similar ecosystems.

20. B: Beetles are insects, which are a type of arthropod. (Arthropoda is the phylum; Insecta is the class.) *Arthropod* means *jointed legs*; this phylum includes many segmented animals with jointed exoskeletons—not only insects but also arachnids (spiders and their relatives), crustaceans (crabs, lobsters, and their kin), and more. Annelids are earthworms and related animals; mollusks include clams, oysters, and octopuses; chordates include any animals with backbones (and a few that don't have backbones but have a precursor of a spinal cord), including humans.

21. B: The energy involved in turning a crank involves motion, so it's *kinetic energy*—the energy in moving objects. Chemical energy comes from chemical reactions, *thermal energy* comes from heat, and *potential energy* is stored energy that can be released later. A book on a high shelf has gravitational potential energy; if it is pushed off the shelf, that potential energy will be converted into kinetic energy as the book falls (and then into thermal and sonic energy when it hits the ground).

22. B: A *conductor* is a material or object that electricity flows through easily, such as a copper wire. An *insulator* is a material or object that does not allow electricity through easily, such as rubber. A *resistor* lets electricity through but impedes its flow somewhat. A *capacitor* is a device consisting of two conducting plates with a thin insulator in between that stores a charge in an electrical circuit.

23. C: The symbol represents an electrical ground, a part of the circuit connected to a large reservoir of charge—often the literal ground of the Earth itself. The main purpose of the electrical ground is to prevent potentially dangerous charges from accumulating due to leaking current or other causes. Any excess charge is harmlessly conducted away into the ground.

The symbols for the other three circuit components mentioned are as follows:

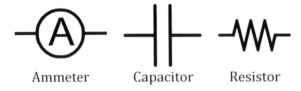

Ammeter   Capacitor   Resistor

24. A: The graph clearly shows the iron content increasing as the river flows—as the distance from the source goes up, so does the iron content. This can best be explained by the river dissolving minerals from the surrounding Earth. While it's true that running rivers also deposit minerals, that would tend to decrease the iron content and wouldn't explain the data in the graph. (Apparently this particular river gains more iron from dissolving minerals than it loses to deposition.)

25. C: The iron content went from 0.6 ppm (parts per million) to 0.68 ppm. That's a change of 0.08 ppm, or as a percentage change, it's $\frac{|0.68-0.6|}{0.6} \approx 0.13 = 13\%$.

26. C: *Evaporation* is the process of liquid water turning into water vapor, and *transpiration* is evaporation of water specifically from plants. Both evaporation and transpiration put water vapor into the atmosphere, so neither could have come immediately before the water's flowing in a river. *Infiltration* is the process of water's soaking into the ground; after infiltration, water becomes groundwater, not river water. *Precipitation* is water falling from clouds in forms such as rain or snow. It's certainly possible for the water in a river to come from precipitation, so this may be the previous step in the water cycle. (It's unlikely that all the water in the river came directly from precipitation, however; the water in the river could also have come in part from *runoff*—water flowing over the surface of the land—or from springs, or melting glaciers, or snow.)

27. B: All the water in, on, and under the planet is collectively called the *hydrosphere*. The *biosphere* is the collective term for all the life on a planet. Panthalassa was the single ocean that existed at a time in prehistory when all the Earth's continents were joined into the single landmass of Pangaea;

Panthalassa did not, however, include rivers and lakes and groundwater. The Seven Seas is a nonscientific term either for specific bodies of water or to refer figuratively to the seas and oceans in general. (Even in the latter meaning, like Panthalassa, it does not refer to water outside the seas and oceans.)

28. C: Major systems of the human body include the circulatory system, the digestive system, the endocrine system, the excretory system, the muscular system, the nervous system, the reproductive system, the respiratory system, and the skeletal system. These systems are sometimes called by different names (i.e., the circulatory system is often called the cardiovascular system), and sometimes other systems are included, such as the immune system, the lymphatic system (often considered part of either the immune system or the cardiovascular system), and the integumentary system (which includes the skin and hair and other external tissues). There is, however, no organ system of the human body conventionally called the regulatory system. While it's true that the human organism, like other organisms, does have to regulate its internal environment in response to internal and external changes, this is a complex process in which many systems play a part: The nervous system detects alterations in the environment, for instance; the endocrine system produces hormones to effect compensatory changes, and so on.

29. A: The circulatory system moves nutrients and chemicals around the body through the blood vessels. The heart is part of the circulatory system, as are all blood vessels—arteries, veins, and capillaries. Because the aorta is an artery, it belongs to the circulatory system.

30. B: The *half-life* is the time it takes for half the substance to decay. If the emission is 2440 MBq on the first day, then half of that amount is 1220 MBq, which should be the approximate amount of the emission after one half-life. The emission is 1218 MBq, which is very close to 1220 MBq, on the fourth day—3 days after the first day. So the half-life must be about 3 days. (Note that 3 days after that, on Day 7, the emission is 611 MBq or about half of 1218.)

31. D: Radioactive decay may result in the emission of *alpha particles*, which comprise two protons and two neutrons, or *beta particles*, which comprise a single electron (or possibly a positron, its antiparticle), or *gamma rays*, high-frequency electromagnetic radiation. *X-rays* do of course exist—they are electromagnetic radiation with a higher frequency than ultraviolet light but not as high as gamma rays—but they do not result from radioactive decay.

32. A: As the fermium radioactively decays, it will lose mass because of the particles it throws off. This rules out Choices C and D. (It's also possible, depending on the kind of radioactive decay, for the mass to remain essentially unchanged, but that doesn't correspond to any of the given choices.) To choose between A and B, note that Choice B has the mass halving every 3 days, matching the radioactive half-life. That would only be true if (1) the sample was initially composed entirely of fermium-253, (2) all of the radioactivity was of a form that depleted the atoms' mass, and (3) when an atom radioactively decayed, its mass completely disappeared. It is uncertain whether (1) and (2) are true, but (3) is certainly false—an atom does not totally disappear when it radioactively decays; its mass is reduced but not to zero. So, Choice B is not realistic, leaving Choice A as the only remaining possibility.

33. A: In about 6 billion years, the Sun, like other stars of its kind, will expand into a red giant star, swallowing all of the inner planets (possibly including the Earth). About a billion years later, it will begin to shrink and cool into a white dwarf. While some stars do explode into supernovas, the Sun is not large enough for this; to undergo a supernova, a star must have at least about eight times the mass of the Sun. After the supernova, the remains of some stars collapse into black holes, but the minimum mass for this to take place is even larger.

34. C: It doesn't make sense to say the moon is closer to space (both the Earth and the moon are in space, of course), and while the Earth's magnetic field does help deflect some of the charged particles radiated from the Sun, it doesn't do anything against meteors. Per unit area, the Earth and the moon are probably hit by about the same number of large meteors. (Small meteors may burn up in the Earth's atmosphere, but meteors massive enough to form large craters are also massive enough to get through the atmosphere without significant reduction.) The main difference is that, with no atmosphere, no running water, and no plate tectonics, the moon's surface doesn't change much; once a crater is there, it's there to stay, and many of the craters on the moon may be millions or even billions of years old. On the Earth, craters won't last nearly that long; they'll be worn down by erosion or carried under the crust by plate tectonics long before then. The few impact craters that do exist on Earth (such as Meteor Crater in Arizona) are still there only because they're very new by geologic timescales, less than a hundred thousand or so years old.

35. B: According to the student's data, the areas with the most bacteria are the cafeteria tables—an especially dangerous place for there to be a lot of bacteria because students eat there! Cleaning the cafeteria tables before meals could cut down on the number of bacteria there, reducing the chances of disease. The actions stated in the other choices could also have a possibility of reducing disease but would be less effective because the other locations have fewer bacteria and are not as likely to contribute to the problem.

36. D: The flu is caused by an airborne virus, not by bacteria. It is usually transmitted through the air from coughs and sneezes. While the flu can also be caught by contaminated surfaces, the student only measured the bacteria on different surfaces, not the viruses. Still, because the flu can be caught by this means, cleanliness and washing hands can help reduce the chances of catching it.

37. B: A large outbreak of disease is called an *epidemic*. An *antibody* is a chemical produced by the body to fight disease, and *immunity* is resistance to disease. *Infection* can refer to a person's catching a disease, but generally is applied on an individual basis, and says nothing about the size of the outbreak.

38. D: From Newton's Second Law of Motion, $F = ma$; if there is a net (unbalanced) force on an object, then it must have a (nonzero) acceleration. This means the object's velocity must be changing. This could be either because the magnitude of the velocity (speed) is changing (either increasing or decreasing) or because the direction of motion is changing—or both.

39. A: An object inherently has a particular mass, which does not change based on the object's surroundings. An object's weight, however, is equal to the force with which gravity pulls on it. On Earth, an object's mass and weight are proportional to each other and more or less interchangeable for many purposes. However, an object's weight will change—but its mass will remain the same—if, for example, it is transported to the moon, where the pull of gravity is smaller.

40. A: Among the earliest life-forms were photosynthetic cyanobacteria, which like most photosynthetic organisms today, took in carbon dioxide and produced oxygen, eventually dramatically increasing the oxygen content in the atmosphere (and paving the way for the eventual development of oxygen-breathing life-forms such as humans). The Sun does not radiate oxygen, and comets and meteors do not bring significant amounts of molecular oxygen either. Volcanic activity does have an effect on the atmosphere but not to increase its oxygen content; volcanoes release primarily carbon dioxide, sulfur dioxide, and water vapor, along with smaller amounts of hydrogen and other gases.

41. C: Fossilization usually occurs when an organism is buried in silt or similar materials; the soft tissues rot away, but the bones or shells are gradually replaced by minerals that become the fossils. The earliest life-forms were soft-bodied organisms that had no bones or shells, so they didn't usually fossilize. Under some circumstances, however, the soft parts of an organism can fossilize, and there are places where such fossils have been found—the Burgess Shale in British Columbia is perhaps the most famous such location. It's largely thanks to unusual places like these that we know as much about very early life-forms as we do.

42. A: A *behavioral response* is a set of actions that an organism performs in response to some internal or external stimulus. In this case, the monkey's seeing the eagle is the stimulus, and the call is the response. Behavioral responses involve coordination of many systems (the nervous system to process what the monkey sees, the muscular and respiratory systems to produce the call, etc.) and may be learned, hereditary, or a combination of both.

43. A: Nonliving components of an ecosystem that affect its ability to support life are called *abiotic*—in contrast to *biotic*, or living, factors. In addition to temperature and water, other abiotic factors might include richness of the soil, light levels, minerals, and so on.

Social Studies

Civics/ Government

1. C: The term "checks and balances" refers to the division of government roles so that no single branch might hold all of the power. The term has nothing to do with economics or budget and, while the Founding Fathers knew that the Constitution was not perfect, there was a provision for amendments to change parts of the document.

2. A: The Great Compromise refers to the agreement to have a bicameral legislature wherein states would have equal representation in the Senate and representation based on state population in the House of Representatives; this compromise was a result of the decision to adopt a document other than the Articles of Confederation. The agreement that a slave would count as three-fifths of a person for purposes of representation and taxation is known as the Three-Fifths Compromise.

3. C: A "veto" refers to the president's constitutional right to reject a bill passed by Congress. While the president has this power, it is not absolute. A veto may be overturned by a two-thirds majority vote in Congress.

4. B: Implied powers are powers not specifically expressed by the Constitution, but that can be inferred from the text. These implied powers are granted by the so-called "Elastic Clause" in Article 1, Section 8 of the Constitution, allowing Congress the power to do whatever is necessary and proper in order to accomplish their duties.

5. B: The administrative system that serves to govern the United States of America is often called the Bureaucracy. A bureaucracy may include the president's cabinet, government staff, aides and many more nonelected government officials.

6. C: The framers of the Constitution used the term "Federalism" to explain the sharing of powers by central and state governments. Alexander Hamilton formed the Federalist Party and John Adams served as the party's only president.

7. B: A lobbyist is another name for a person seeking to influence an elected official on a particular issue. A constituent is a voting member of a community, a delegate is a person authorized to represent constituents at political conventions, and an incumbent is the elected official currently holding office.

8. A: Judicial review is the right of federal courts to determine if a law passed by Congress violates the Constitution. Once a Supreme Court justice has been installed, he or she can only be removed by resignation or death. Furthermore, the Supreme Court does not have the power to revoke the office of politicians.

9. A: The sitting president is responsible for appointing Supreme Court judges. Once the president appoints a nominee, the responsibility falls upon Congress to confirm the appointment.

10. C: A filibuster is the act of a member of congress giving long speeches in order to block the passage of certain legislation. This is distinct from gerrymandering, which refers to drawing electoral districts that provide a political advantage to a certain party; muckraking, which refers to investigative journalists; and pork barrel, which is a means for funneling money to a politician's home district.

11. B: Political parties do not manage the day-to-day operations of the military. The military is under the direct leadership of the executive branch of government, and, as such, the sitting president of the United States.

12. A: Concurrent powers are powers granted by the Constitution that are shared by both state and federal governments. Concurrent powers include the power to tax and the power to maintain road systems.

13. A: The 10th Amendment grants reserved powers to the states. This amendment is the reason for the disparity between state laws regarding issues such as gay marriage and legalization of cannabis.

14. D: The vice president's religious beliefs will not affect the religious freedoms of the people. However, the vice president is an important person because he is responsible for providing the deciding vote in the event of a tie vote in the Senate, serving as a diplomat to other heads of state, and assuming presidential roles in the event that the sitting president is unable to serve.

Geography

1. C: The Ural mountain range separates Europe from Asia. The Blue Ridge Mountains are a part of the Appalachian Mountain Range in the eastern United States of America, while the Alps and the Pyrenees separate nations inside of Europe.

2. C: Laos is not an African nation; it is located in Southeast Asia. Morocco, Togo, and Mozambique span the continent of Africa from northwest to southeast.

3. A: A canal is an artificial waterway used as a channel for water. There are two main types of canals: waterways and aqueducts. Waterways are used to navigate ships, while aqueducts are used to transport water for consumption. Conversely, ponds, creeks, and rivers all exist naturally around the world.

4. D: The Suez Canal is located in Egypt. This canal, opened in 1869, connects the Mediterranean Sea with the Red Sea. This route allows for ships to travel between Europe and Asia without travelling around Africa. Meanwhile, the nations of Chad, Czech Republic, and Bolivia are landlocked.

5. B: Turkey is not a member nation of the European Union. The European Union consists of Austria, Belgium, Bulgaria, Croatia, Cyprus, Czech Republic, Denmark, Estonia, Finland, France, Germany, Greece, Hungary, Ireland, Italy, Latvia, Lithuania, Luxembourg, Malta, the Netherlands, Poland, Portugal, Romania, Slovakia, Slovenia, Spain, Sweden, and the United Kingdom.

6. A: India, being a distinguishable part of the Asian continent, is defined as a subcontinent. Madagascar, Australia, and Greenland are all islands, and thus incapable of being designated as subcontinents.

7. D: Australia is both a country and a continent. Canada and Russia, while massive, are parts of their continents North America, and Europe and Asia, respectively. Greenland, while an island, is neither its own continent nor its own country, as it is an autonomous country within the Kingdom of Denmark.

8. C: Poland was never a part of the Republic of the Soviet Union. The former Republic of the Soviet Union consisted of Russia, Ukraine, Uzbekistan, Kazakhstan, Belarus, Azerbaijan, Georgia, Tajikistan, Moldova, Kyrgyzstan, Lithuania, Turkmenistan, Armenia, Latvia, and Estonia.

9. A: Uruguay is the only country that is actually in South America. Nicaragua, Belize, and El Salvador are all a part of Central America, and as such, are classified as North American nations.

History

1. B: The Magna Carta declared that English citizens were free from punishment except through established law. The United States of America declared its independence in the 1776 document, the Declaration of Independence. The American people were granted the right to religious freedom and freedom of speech by the 1787 document, the Constitution of United States.

2. D: The French and Indian War was not a main reason for the American Revolution. While the French and Indian War heighted tensions, it would be more than a decade after the end of the French and Indian War before the American Revolution erupted.

3. C: Harriet Beecher Stowe's Uncle Tom's Cabin was not a direct result of the end of slavery in the United States. In fact, the book was released more than a decade prior to the abolition of slavery in the United States, serving to highlight the injustice of American slavery.

4. A: Nebraska was still a territory during the Civil War, not joining the union until 1867. Tennessee, Texas, and Wisconsin joined the union earlier, in the years 1796, 1845, and 1848, respectively.

5. B: The assassination of Archduke Franz Ferdinand of Austria-Hungary triggered the First World War. The Seven Years' War fought between France and England on two continents was triggered by both nations' need to expand. The Austro-Prussian War was caused by the Prussians' plan to expel Austria from the German Confederation. Lastly, World War II was caused by, among other things, an aggressive Germany.

6. C: The Allied Forces were composed of the Great Britain, the Soviet Union, Australia, and the United States, along with many other nations. Switzerland remained neutral throughout the war. The Axis powers consisted of Italy, Germany, and Japan, among others.

7. A: Nationalism was a driving force in the militant nature of multiple nations, most notably Germany and Italy. While fascist dictators led both of these nations, it was nationalism that served as a unifying catalyst to war.

8. D: Benito Mussolini was the leader of Italy's National Fascist Party preceding and during World War II. This is distinct from the National Socialist Party in Germany at the time that was led by Adolf Hitler. While both Mussolini and Hitler were fascists, Joseph Stalin and Leon Trotsky were ardent communists, situated on the exact opposite side of the political spectrum.

9. D: The California Gold Rush had an enormous impact on the western United States. The rise in population was unprecedented for the area, causing both a rise in the development of travel and a displacement of native peoples. All of the above is the correct answer.

10. D: Children learned in a variety of ways. The most common way in which frontier children were educated was simply by their families at home. Once communities began to develop, a teacher would instruct inside a small schoolhouse when the season permitted. And lastly, once the child surpassed what education could be received through means directly available to them, they would send away for materials and learn by correspondence. The answer is all of the above.

Economics

1. B: In the event that the cost of South American coffee beans rises, companies like Starbucks would raise their prices to accommodate for the new cost. It is highly unlikely that Americans would switch to drinking tea or that the United States would boycott South American nations.

2. A: Antitrust laws are put in place to promote free competition in the marketplace by disrupting the formation of monopolies. A monopoly exists where one entity has exclusive control over a business involving a commodity or service.

3. D: The Federal Trade Commission (FTC) is responsible for protecting consumers while maintaining free and fair competition in the marketplace. The Internal Revenue Service is best known for their governance over taxes. The Environmental Protection Agency is, as the name implies, an agency devoted to protecting the environment. The Federal Bureau of Investigation deals with criminal investigations across the nation.

4. C: A bond is a certificate issued by a borrower that promises to repay lender money at a fixed interest rate. Essentially, a bond is an IOU traditionally issued by credible institutions and governments.

5. B: Entrepreneurism refers to the organization, management, and risk of a business taken on by an individual. It does not necessarily mean the first business to enter a new market or industry.

6. D: Sources of revenue are divided into two categories: tax revenue and non-tax revenue. Taxes fall under tax revenue, while loans, fines and penalties constitute non-tax revenues. The correct answer, then, is all of the above.

7. D: Making loans at interest is a service provided by almost all banks and credit unions. The Federal Reserve, which also distributes currency to the United States Treasury Department which then prints new currency, is responsible for setting interest rates in the United States.

8. B: The government's primary purpose behind the prevention of monopolies is to encourage a competitive market. By encouraging a competitive market, the government seeks to stimulate economic growth.

9. D: The Federal Reserve carries out the United States of America's monetary policy. The Ways and Means Committee is responsible for raising revenue within the United States government, while the Internal Revenue Service is responsible for collecting revenue.

10. C: The downturn of economies across the world following the 2008 recession in the United States is an example of the interdependence of the world market. There are other currencies in the world that are strong and one can predict with some certainty how economies may respond to each other; however, the global economy is interconnected, now more than ever.

Vocabulary

1. D: private

2. D: building airplanes and rockets

3. B: fine plaster

4. C: like an angry child

5. A: refuse to shop there

6. B: important period of time

7. C: believable

8. D: a person who's superior to others

9. A: extraordinary

10. C: modern

11. A: turn away

12. D: unusual

13. B: unfriendly

14. B: full of tiny holes

15. C: efforts

16. D: short passage from

17. A: a sculpture or doll resembling a person

18. B: easily irritated

19. C: talk about the past

20. B: make very important

21. A: loud and harsh

22. D: complicated

23. C: bravery

24. A: sad poem at a funeral

25. D: say bad things about

26. B: a great number

27. C: spur of the moment

28. A: impossible to remove

29. B: an object to remind one of something

30. A: area

31. C: can be touched

32. B: speed

33. A: source of strength

34. C: loud and unruly

35. D: irregular

36. B: bold

37. B: false name

38. A: list

39. C: fancy

40. B: be very hot

41. D: contempt

42. B: transport

Spelling

1. arroneous – this should be erroneous

2. hazzard – this should be hazard

3. morgage – this should be mortgage

4. resede – this should be recede

5. sentimeter – this should be centimeter

6. mischievious – this should be mischievous

7. mersonary – this should be mercenary

8. comemorate – this should be commemorate

9. connasewer – this should be connoisseur

10. *sermise* – this should be *surmise*

11. coladeral – this should be collateral

12. narrater – this should be narrator

13. meticulus – this should be meticulous

14. qwixotic – this should be quixotic

15. *jurer* – this should be *juror*

16. grotesk – this should be grotesque

17. dillemma – this should be dilemma

18. *undooly* – this should be *unduly*

19. *malody* – this should be *malady*

20. *abstane* – this should be *abstain*

21. ashphalt – this should be asphalt

22. anikdote – this should be anecdote

23. *vetaran* – this should be *veteran*

24. eccessive – this should be excessive

25. *oncore* – this should be *encore*

26. acumulate – this should be accumulate

27. deffective – this should be defective

28. *eddible* – this should be *edible*

29. comerse – this should be commerce

30. cinamun – this should be cinnamon

31. arkeology – this should be archaeology

32. corperal – this should be corporal

33. jenuine – this should be genuine

34. devinity – this should be divinity

35. borometer – this should be barometer

Capitalization

1. A: Ben Franklin said, "early to bed, early to rise, makes a man healthy, wealthy and wise."

Should be: *Ben Franklin said, "Early to bed, early to rise, makes a man healthy, wealthy and wise."*

2. B: Didn't your Father attend college in Europe, Wendell?

Should be: *Didn't your father attend college in Europe, Wendell?*

3. C: My older brother is thinking about enrolling in a Community College.

Should be: *My older brother is thinking about enrolling in a community college.*

4. B: Popular Breeds of dogs include German Shepherds, Labrador Retrievers, and Boxers.

Should be: *Popular breeds of dogs include German Shepherds, Labrador Retrievers, and Boxers.*

5. B: The halloween party for the class will be this Friday, kids.

Should be: *The Halloween party for the class will be this Friday, kids.*

6. A: Sally said her Mom will pick her up after practice is over.

Should be: *Sally said her mom will pick her up after practice is over.*

7. C: The statue of liberty is one of the top attractions in the City.

Should be: *The Statue of Liberty is one of the top attractions in the city.*

8. C: Hey, Steve, this Summer let's visit the Rocky Mountains.

Should be: *Hey, Steve, this summer let's visit the Rocky Mountains.*

9. C: If you ask me, nfl players make way too much money.

Should be: *If you ask me, NFL players make way too much money.*

10. A: I don't like Algebra, but I like history and social studies.

Should be: *I don't like algebra, but I like history and social studies.*

11. B: I heard that algebra 2 is very hard to get an A in.

Should be: *I heard that Algebra 2 is very hard to get an A in.*

12. B: They call New York City the big apple for a very good reason!

Should be: *They call New York City the Big Apple for a very good reason!*

13. C: The Capital of the European country of France is Paris.

Should be: *The capital of the European country of France is Paris.*

14. A: Mercury, Mars, and Venus are the smallest of all the Planets.

Should be: *Mercury, Mars, and Venus are the smallest of all the planets.*

15. C: I saw my first broadway play last year on our class trip.

Should be: *I saw my first Broadway play last year on our class trip.*

16. A: The whole family sang "happy birthday" at the top of our lungs!

Should be: The whole family sang "Happy Birthday" at the top of our lungs!

17. A: President Obama will arrive soon on his plane, air force one.

Should be: *President Obama will arrive soon on his plane, Air Force One.*

18. C: I wrote to my Congressman about out of control Federal Spending.

Should be: *I wrote to my Congressman about out of control federal spending.*

19. NO MISTAKES

20. C: Aunt Ramona said her Uncle is 100 years old.

Should be: *Aunt Ramona said her uncle is 100 years old.*

21. B: We saw an antique Ford model t on display there.

Should be: *We saw an antique Ford Model T on display there.*

22. A: One of my favorite breakfast meals is eggs benedict.

Should be: *One of my favorite breakfast meals is Eggs Benedict.*

23. C: Jimmy I both like Pancakes, and we both like Sausage.

Should be: *Jimmy I both like pancakes, and we both like sausage.*

24. A: Cook county is where Chicago, Illinois, is located.

Should be: *Cook County is where Chicago, Illinois, is located.*

25. B: The Army, Air Force, Navy, and Marines are all military Organizations.

Should be: *The Army, Air Force, Navy, and Marines are all military organizations.*

26. A: "The Wind in the willows" is one of the best books I have ever read.

Should be: *"The Wind in the Willows" is one of the best books I have ever read.*

27. C: My dad once ate an entire Pepperoni Pizza by himself!

Should be: *My dad once ate an entire pepperoni pizza by himself!*

129

28. A: Dear Mom and Dad, congratulations on your upcoming Anniversary!

Should be: *Dear Mom and Dad, congratulations on your upcoming anniversary!*

29. B: New Orleans is famous for its Jazz Music.

Should be: *New Orleans is famous for its jazz music.*

Punctuation

1. A: We'll be visiting Boston, and New York City.

Should be: *We'll be visiting Boston and New York City.*

2. B: The dog, eager for a walk brought his leash to his master.

Should be: *The dog, eager for a walk, brought his leash to his master.*

3. B: We need eggs; milk; and bread.

Should be: *We need eggs, milk, and bread.*

4. C: Theres no time like the present for making changes.

Should be: *There's no time like the present for making changes.*

5. A: The kitten loves to chase it's tail.

Should be: *The kitten loves to chase its tail.*

6. B: Mrs. Smiths' cat had six kittens last night.

Should be: *Mrs. Smith's cat had six kittens last night.*

7. B: This is my little brother – Tommy.

Should be: *This is my little brother, Tommy.*

8. A: He asked, "Mom, do you need any help with the groceries"?

Should be: He asked, "Mom, do you need any help with the groceries?"

9. A: Robert; would you please mail this letter for me?

Should be: *Robert, would you please mail this letter for me?*

10. B: Hermione, that's a terrific idea:

Should be: *Hermione, that's a terrific idea.*

11. B: He hit the ball and ran very-quickly toward first base.

Should be: *He hit the ball and ran very quickly toward first base.*

12. A: I believe Americas best days are still to come.

Should be: *I believe America's best days are still to come.*

13. A: Edgar Allan Poe was one of the greatest poet's who ever lived.

Should be: *Edgar Allan Poe was one of the greatest poets who ever lived.*

14. C: 3 time's 15 equals 45.

Should be: *3 times 15 equals 45.*

15. D: NO MISTAKES

16. A: What does "one if by land, and two if by sea", mean?

Should be: *What does "one if by land, and two if by sea" mean?*

17. C: My mother (and father) have been married for 15 years.

Should be: *My mother and father have been married for 15 years.*

18. B: The Jones's front lawn earned them a city beautification award last year.

Should be: *The Jones' front lawn earned them a city beautification award last year.*

19. C: That new song is the cats meow.

Should be: *That new song is the cat's meow.*

20. A: If you break it; you must replace it.

Should be: *If you break it, you must replace it.*

21. C: The paper "described the plaintiff" as being very satisfied with the settlement.

Should be: *The paper described the plaintiff as being very satisfied with the settlement.*

22. A: The hippopotamus, and the elephant, are two of the biggest land animals.

Should be: *The hippopotamus and the elephant are two of the biggest land animals.*

23. B: After 20 losses in a row, its about time to hire a new coach.

Should be: *After 20 losses in a row, it's about time to hire a new coach.*

24. C: All, aboard!

Should be: *All aboard!*

25. B: Frank loves his mom's cooking, his favorite dessert is her apple pie.

Should be: *Frank loves his mom's cooking; his favorite dessert is her apple pie.*

26. B: I like pizza, more than hamburgers.

Should be: *I like pizza more than hamburgers.*

27. A: Take two aspirin: and call me in the morning.

Should be: *Take two aspirin and call me in the morning.*

28. B: I can't believe I got a ticket on my bicycle for ignoring a "stop sign."

Should be: *I can't believe I got a ticket on my bicycle for ignoring a stop sign.*

29. C: I had no idea that wedding-cakes are so expensive.

Should be: *I had no idea that wedding cakes are so expensive.*

How to Overcome Test Anxiety

Just the thought of taking a test is enough to make most people a little nervous. A test is an important event that can have a long-term impact on your future, so it's important to take it seriously and it's natural to feel anxious about performing well. But just because anxiety is normal, that doesn't mean that it's helpful in test taking, or that you should simply accept it as part of your life. Anxiety can have a variety of effects. These effects can be mild, like making you feel slightly nervous, or severe, like blocking your ability to focus or remember even a simple detail.

If you experience test anxiety—whether severe or mild—it's important to know how to beat it. To discover this, first you need to understand what causes test anxiety.

Causes of Test Anxiety

While we often think of anxiety as an uncontrollable emotional state, it can actually be caused by simple, practical things. One of the most common causes of test anxiety is that a person does not feel adequately prepared for their test. This feeling can be the result of many different issues such as poor study habits or lack of organization, but the most common culprit is time management. Starting to study too late, failing to organize your study time to cover all of the material, or being distracted while you study will mean that you're not well prepared for the test. This may lead to cramming the night before, which will cause you to be physically and mentally exhausted for the test. Poor time management also contributes to feelings of stress, fear, and hopelessness as you realize you are not well prepared but don't know what to do about it.

Other times, test anxiety is not related to your preparation for the test but comes from unresolved fear. This may be a past failure on a test, or poor performance on tests in general. It may come from comparing yourself to others who seem to be performing better or from the stress of living up to expectations. Anxiety may be driven by fears of the future—how failure on this test would affect your educational and career goals. These fears are often completely irrational, but they can still negatively impact your test performance.

Elements of Test Anxiety

As mentioned earlier, test anxiety is considered to be an emotional state, but it has physical and mental components as well. Sometimes you may not even realize that you are suffering from test anxiety until you notice the physical symptoms. These can include trembling hands, rapid heartbeat, sweating, nausea, and tense muscles. Extreme anxiety may lead to fainting or vomiting. Obviously, any of these symptoms can have a negative impact on testing. It is important to recognize them as soon as they begin to occur so that you can address the problem before it damages your performance.

The mental components of test anxiety include trouble focusing and inability to remember learned information. During a test, your mind is on high alert, which can help you recall information and stay focused for an extended period of time. However, anxiety interferes with your mind's natural processes, causing you to blank out, even on the questions you know well. The strain of testing during anxiety makes it difficult to stay focused, especially on a test that may take several hours. Extreme anxiety can take a huge mental toll, making it difficult not only to recall test information but even to understand the test questions or pull your thoughts together.

Effects of Test Anxiety

Test anxiety is like a disease—if left untreated, it will get progressively worse. Anxiety leads to poor performance, and this reinforces the feelings of fear and failure, which in turn lead to poor performances on subsequent tests. It can grow from a mild nervousness to a crippling condition. If allowed to progress, test anxiety can have a big impact on your schooling, and consequently on your future.

Test anxiety can spread to other parts of your life. Anxiety on tests can become anxiety in any stressful situation, and blanking on a test can turn into panicking in a job situation. But fortunately, you don't have to let anxiety rule your testing and determine your grades. There are a number of relatively simple steps you can take to move past anxiety and function normally on a test and in the rest of life.

Physical Steps for Beating Test Anxiety

While test anxiety is a serious problem, the good news is that it can be overcome. It doesn't have to control your ability to think and remember information. While it may take time, you can begin taking steps today to beat anxiety.

Just as your first hint that you may be struggling with anxiety comes from the physical symptoms, the first step to treating it is also physical. Rest is crucial for having a clear, strong mind. If you are tired, it is much easier to give in to anxiety. But if you establish good sleep habits, your body and mind will be ready to perform optimally, without the strain of exhaustion. Additionally, sleeping well helps you to retain information better, so you're more likely to recall the answers when you see the test questions.

Getting good sleep means more than going to bed on time. It's important to allow your brain time to relax. Take study breaks from time to time so it doesn't get overworked, and don't study right before bed. Take time to rest your mind before trying to rest your body, or you may find it difficult to fall asleep.

Along with sleep, other aspects of physical health are important in preparing for a test. Good nutrition is vital for good brain function. Sugary foods and drinks may give a burst of energy but this burst is followed by a crash, both physically and emotionally. Instead, fuel your body with protein and vitamin-rich foods.

Also, drink plenty of water. Dehydration can lead to headaches and exhaustion, especially if your brain is already under stress from the rigors of the test. Particularly if your test is a long one, drink water during the breaks. And if possible, take an energy-boosting snack to eat between sections.

Along with sleep and diet, a third important part of physical health is exercise. Maintaining a steady workout schedule is helpful, but even taking 5-minute study breaks to walk can help get your blood pumping faster and clear your head. Exercise also releases endorphins, which contribute to a positive feeling and can help combat test anxiety.

When you nurture your physical health, you are also contributing to your mental health. If your body is healthy, your mind is much more likely to be healthy as well. So take time to rest, nourish your body with healthy food and water, and get moving as much as possible. Taking these physical steps will make you stronger and more able to take the mental steps necessary to overcome test anxiety.

Mental Steps for Beating Test Anxiety

Working on the mental side of test anxiety can be more challenging, but as with the physical side, there are clear steps you can take to overcome it. As mentioned earlier, test anxiety often stems from lack of preparation, so the obvious solution is to prepare for the test. Effective studying may be the most important weapon you have for beating test anxiety, but you can and should employ several other mental tools to combat fear.

First, boost your confidence by reminding yourself of past success—tests or projects that you aced. If you're putting as much effort into preparing for this test as you did for those, there's no reason you should expect to fail here. Work hard to prepare; then trust your preparation.

Second, surround yourself with encouraging people. It can be helpful to find a study group, but be sure that the people you're around will encourage a positive attitude. If you spend time with others who are anxious or cynical, this will only contribute to your own anxiety. Look for others who are motivated to study hard from a desire to succeed, not from a fear of failure.

Third, reward yourself. A test is physically and mentally tiring, even without anxiety, and it can be helpful to have something to look forward to. Plan an activity following the test, regardless of the outcome, such as going to a movie or getting ice cream.

When you are taking the test, if you find yourself beginning to feel anxious, remind yourself that you know the material. Visualize successfully completing the test. Then take a few deep, relaxing breaths and return to it. Work through the questions carefully but with confidence, knowing that you are capable of succeeding.

Developing a healthy mental approach to test taking will also aid in other areas of life. Test anxiety affects more than just the actual test—it can be damaging to your mental health and even contribute to depression. It's important to beat test anxiety before it becomes a problem for more than testing.

Study Strategy

Being prepared for the test is necessary to combat anxiety, but what does being prepared look like? You may study for hours on end and still not feel prepared. What you need is a strategy for test prep. The next few pages outline our recommended steps to help you plan out and conquer the challenge of preparation.

STEP 1: SCOPE OUT THE TEST

Learn everything you can about the format (multiple choice, essay, etc.) and what will be on the test. Gather any study materials, course outlines, or sample exams that may be available. Not only will this help you to prepare, but knowing what to expect can help to alleviate test anxiety.

STEP 2: MAP OUT THE MATERIAL

Look through the textbook or study guide and make note of how many chapters or sections it has. Then divide these over the time you have. For example, if a book has 15 chapters and you have five days to study, you need to cover three chapters each day. Even better, if you have the time, leave an extra day at the end for overall review after you have gone through the material in depth.

If time is limited, you may need to prioritize the material. Look through it and make note of which sections you think you already have a good grasp on, and which need review. While you are studying, skim quickly through the familiar sections and take more time on the challenging parts.

Write out your plan so you don't get lost as you go. Having a written plan also helps you feel more in control of the study, so anxiety is less likely to arise from feeling overwhelmed at the amount to cover.

STEP 3: GATHER YOUR TOOLS

Decide what study method works best for you. Do you prefer to highlight in the book as you study and then go back over the highlighted portions? Or do you type out notes of the important information? Or is it helpful to make flashcards that you can carry with you? Assemble the pens, index cards, highlighters, post-it notes, and any other materials you may need so you won't be distracted by getting up to find things while you study.

If you're having a hard time retaining the information or organizing your notes, experiment with different methods. For example, try color-coding by subject with colored pens, highlighters, or post-it notes. If you learn better by hearing, try recording yourself reading your notes so you can listen while in the car, working out, or simply sitting at your desk. Ask a friend to quiz you from your flashcards, or try teaching someone the material to solidify it in your mind.

STEP 4: CREATE YOUR ENVIRONMENT

It's important to avoid distractions while you study. This includes both the obvious distractions like visitors and the subtle distractions like an uncomfortable chair (or a too-comfortable couch that makes you want to fall asleep). Set up the best study environment possible: good lighting and a comfortable work area. If background music helps you focus, you may want to turn it on, but otherwise keep the room quiet. If you are using a computer to take notes, be sure you don't have any other windows open, especially applications like social media, games, or anything else that could distract you. Silence your phone and turn off notifications. Be sure to keep water close by so you stay hydrated while you study (but avoid unhealthy drinks and snacks).

Also, take into account the best time of day to study. Are you freshest first thing in the morning? Try to set aside some time then to work through the material. Is your mind clearer in the afternoon or evening? Schedule your study session then. Another method is to study at the same time of day that you will take the test, so that your brain gets used to working on the material at that time and will be ready to focus at test time.

STEP 5: STUDY!

Once you have done all the study preparation, it's time to settle into the actual studying. Sit down, take a few moments to settle your mind so you can focus, and begin to follow your study plan. Don't give in to distractions or let yourself procrastinate. This is your time to prepare so you'll be ready to fearlessly approach the test. Make the most of the time and stay focused.

Of course, you don't want to burn out. If you study too long you may find that you're not retaining the information very well. Take regular study breaks. For example, taking five minutes out of every hour to walk briskly, breathing deeply and swinging your arms, can help your mind stay fresh.

As you get to the end of each chapter or section, it's a good idea to do a quick review. Remind yourself of what you learned and work on any difficult parts. When you feel that you've mastered the material, move on to the next part. At the end of your study session, briefly skim through your notes again.

But while review is helpful, cramming last minute is NOT. If at all possible, work ahead so that you won't need to fit all your study into the last day. Cramming overloads your brain with more information than it can process and retain, and your tired mind may struggle to recall even previously learned information when it is overwhelmed with last-minute study. Also, the urgent nature of cramming and the stress placed on your brain contribute to anxiety. You'll be more likely to go to the test feeling unprepared and having trouble thinking clearly.

So don't cram, and don't stay up late before the test, even just to review your notes at a leisurely pace. Your brain needs rest more than it needs to go over the information again. In fact, plan to finish your studies by noon or early afternoon the day before the test. Give your brain the rest of the day to relax or focus on other things, and get a good night's sleep. Then you will be fresh for the test and better able to recall what you've studied.

STEP 6: TAKE A PRACTICE TEST

Many courses offer sample tests, either online or in the study materials. This is an excellent resource to check whether you have mastered the material, as well as to prepare for the test format and environment.

Check the test format ahead of time: the number of questions, the type (multiple choice, free response, etc.), and the time limit. Then create a plan for working through them. For example, if you have 30 minutes to take a 60-question test, your limit is 30 seconds per question. Spend less time on the questions you know well so that you can take more time on the difficult ones.

If you have time to take several practice tests, take the first one open book, with no time limit. Work through the questions at your own pace and make sure you fully understand them. Gradually work up to taking a test under test conditions: sit at a desk with all study materials put away and set a timer. Pace yourself to make sure you finish the test with time to spare and go back to check your answers if you have time.

After each test, check your answers. On the questions you missed, be sure you understand why you missed them. Did you misread the question (tests can use tricky wording)? Did you forget the information? Or was it something you hadn't learned? Go back and study any shaky areas that the practice tests reveal.

Taking these tests not only helps with your grade, but also aids in combating test anxiety. If you're already used to the test conditions, you're less likely to worry about it, and working through tests until you're scoring well gives you a confidence boost. Go through the practice tests until you feel comfortable, and then you can go into the test knowing that you're ready for it.

Test Tips

On test day, you should be confident, knowing that you've prepared well and are ready to answer the questions. But aside from preparation, there are several test day strategies you can employ to maximize your performance.

First, as stated before, get a good night's sleep the night before the test (and for several nights before that, if possible). Go into the test with a fresh, alert mind rather than staying up late to study.

Try not to change too much about your normal routine on the day of the test. It's important to eat a nutritious breakfast, but if you normally don't eat breakfast at all, consider eating just a protein bar. If you're a coffee drinker, go ahead and have your normal coffee. Just make sure you time it so that the caffeine doesn't wear off right in the middle of your test. Avoid sugary beverages, and drink enough water to stay hydrated but not so much that you need a restroom break 10 minutes into the test. If your test isn't first thing in the morning, consider going for a walk or doing a light workout before the test to get your blood flowing.

Allow yourself enough time to get ready, and leave for the test with plenty of time to spare so you won't have the anxiety of scrambling to arrive in time. Another reason to be early is to select a good seat. It's helpful to sit away from doors and windows, which can be distracting. Find a good seat, get out your supplies, and settle your mind before the test begins.

When the test begins, start by going over the instructions carefully, even if you already know what to expect. Make sure you avoid any careless mistakes by following the directions.

Then begin working through the questions, pacing yourself as you've practiced. If you're not sure on an answer, don't spend too much time on it, and don't let it shake your confidence. Either skip it and come back later, or eliminate as many wrong answers as possible and guess among the remaining ones. Don't dwell on these questions as you continue—put them out of your mind and focus on what lies ahead.

Be sure to read all of the answer choices, even if you're sure the first one is the right answer. Sometimes you'll find a better one if you keep reading. But don't second-guess yourself if you do immediately know the answer. Your gut instinct is usually right. Don't let test anxiety rob you of the information you know.

If you have time at the end of the test (and if the test format allows), go back and review your answers. Be cautious about changing any, since your first instinct tends to be correct, but make sure you didn't misread any of the questions or accidentally mark the wrong answer choice. Look over any you skipped and make an educated guess.

At the end, leave the test feeling confident. You've done your best, so don't waste time worrying about your performance or wishing you could change anything. Instead, celebrate the successful completion of this test. And finally, use this test to learn how to deal with anxiety even better next time.

> **Review Video: Test Anxiety**
> Visit mometrix.com/academy and enter code: 100340

Important Qualification

Not all anxiety is created equal. If your test anxiety is causing major issues in your life beyond the classroom or testing center, or if you are experiencing troubling physical symptoms related to your anxiety, it may be a sign of a serious physiological or psychological condition. If this sounds like your situation, we strongly encourage you to seek professional help.

Additional Bonus Material

Due to our efforts to try to keep this book to a manageable length, we've created a link that will give you access to all of your additional bonus material:

mometrix.com/bonus948/iowal14g8